APR 13 1994

DU

*An
African American's
View*

Brown

vs.

Topeka:

*Desegregation and Miseducation
by Pansye Atkinson*

African American Images
Chicago, Illinois

Cover Graphics by Harcom

Photo Credits: Bettman

First edition, first printing

DEDICATION

To my daughters,
Dianne and Kimberly,
and their children
William Burk and Genelle Nicole,
and all the children of the future.

TABLE OF CONTENTS

TABLE OF CONTENTS

CONTINUED

ACKNOWLEDGMENTS

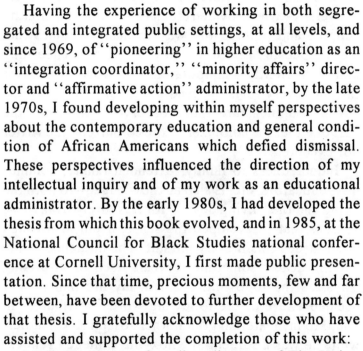

Having the experience of working in both segregated and integrated public settings, at all levels, and since 1969, of "pioneering" in higher education as an "integration coordinator," "minority affairs" director and "affirmative action" administrator, by the late 1970s, I found developing within myself perspectives about the contemporary education and general condition of African Americans which defied dismissal. These perspectives influenced the direction of my intellectual inquiry and of my work as an educational administrator. By the early 1980s, I had developed the thesis from which this book evolved, and in 1985, at the National Council for Black Studies national conference at Cornell University, I first made public presentation. Since that time, precious moments, few and far between, have been devoted to further development of that thesis. I gratefully acknowledge those who have assisted and supported the completion of this work:

Mark Rosenman, founding director of The Union Institute Center for Public Policy, who reviewed an early manuscript and urged continued development of what he termed "important" work; Sylvia Hill, of the Union Institute Graduate School Faculty, who recognized the "passion" with which I pursued my writing and suggested that I develop the early manuscript into a book; political sociologist Manning Marable and legal scholar and former NAACP attorney Derrick Bell, who offered encouraging words as I toiled to produce a completed manuscript; Nancy L. Arnez, Professor in the Howard University School of Education, who painstakingly critiqued the manuscript through its early stages of development; poet, African American Studies scholar, and veritable bibliophile, Fred L. Hord--a former colleague at Frostburg State University--who provided crucial advice and unfaltering support and pointed the way to many volumes that were especially useful; Shelley Drees, who cheerfully and expediently manipulated the word processor through every revision. And not among the least due acknowledgment are those observed acting out the part of either the colonizer or the colonized--the writer not excepted.

Indebtedness to family, extended family, community, educators, etc. is also acknowledged--to both the living and the "living dead," for it is surely from these sources that I developed the sense of purpose which undergirded this literary pursuit. The influence of the "living dead" sometimes reveals itself in surprising ways, as the following event in my life indicates. I became aware of the following words--attributed, in 1883, to my maternal grandfather Joseph A. Chandler, while he was a student at Knoxville College (Tennessee)--one hundred years after they were printed in the campus literary magazine *Aurora:*

> "Every man and every woman should have a purpose in life and that purpose should be such as to call forth work that shall live when the doer is no more. Life is uncertain and death is sure and our work in this life should have good effect upon future generations."

Although I never knew my grandfather, who died at an early age, those words revealed to me much about him and the legacy he afforded me, as well as the sense of purpose with which he went on to pioneer in the field of higher education for African Americans as president of Greeneville Normal and Industrial College in Tennessee (a small institution, which did not survive the Depression of the 1930s, founded in 1889 by the African Methodist Episcopal Zion Church). In addition to my grandfather, acknowledgment is due his wife Ophelia--my grandmother--whom I also never knew, who worked with him as an "instructress" in the institution and later as an educator in Asheville, North Carolina after my grandfather's death; my mother Helen, who was a versatile educator and musician; and my father John E. Smith, a master builder.

Extended family and educators are too numerous to mention, although they have played significant roles, nurturing and helping to shape the values that led to the intellectual and spiritual inquiry which informed my writing. But, I must at least mention some of those who willingly became my "mothers" and "fathers" when that need arose at an early age: my foster parents, Garland E. (now deceased) and Vivian Cline Cooper; my uncle, Harold B. Chandler, and his wife Sarah; my husband's mother, Leola Atkinson Beck.

With one spirit--with like mind--my husband, the late William Reeder Atkinson and I together accepted the challenge in 1969 to assist Frostburg State College (now Frostburg State University) in integration/desegregation efforts (that is a story in itself) and the legacy of his perspective and pursuits is clearly fixed in my mind. So it is that I acknowledge his contribution to this current work.

. . . stand fast in one spirit, with one mind striving together
. . . and in nothing terrified by your adversaries:
which is to them an evident token of perdition,
but to you of salvation,
and that of God.

Philippians 1;27, 28

FOREWORD

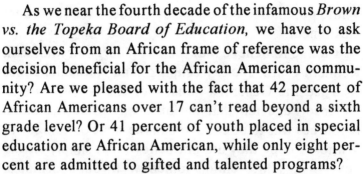

As we near the fourth decade of the infamous *Brown vs. the Topeka Board of Education*, we have to ask ourselves from an African frame of reference was the decision beneficial for the African American community? Are we pleased with the fact that 42 percent of African Americans over 17 can't read beyond a sixth grade level? Or 41 percent of youth placed in special education are African American, while only eight percent are admitted to gifted and talented programs?

African American male students constitute only eight percent of all public school students, but are 37 percent of the students suspended. Often times, they commit the same infraction as white males, but the latter group receives less enforcement. Are we satisfied that in most large urban areas, where 85 percent of the African American community resides, the dropout rate hovers near 50 percent?

The answer should be obvious that desegregation has not enhanced the academic achievement of African American youth. The initial logic was that the schools were separate and unequal. Jonathon Kozol points out in *Savage Inequalities*, forty years later, schools are still separate and unequal. Schools predominantly in majority White suburbs have a per-pupil expenditure averaging $13,000 while in the African American inner-city, the average is a deplorable $5,000. *Brown vs. Topeka* has created White flight and the further development of White private schools. In cities across America, the student population of people of color far exceeds the White population. In two of the most racist cities in the country, Chicago and Boston, the following examples are provided for illumination. Chicago has a 45 percent White population but only a 15 percent White student enrollment. Boston has a 75 percent White population but only a 35 percent White student enrollment.

I'd like to believe that the late Thurgood Marshall, Kenneth Clark, Jack Greenburg, and Nathaniel Jones who led the General Counsel for the NAACP Legal Defense Fund felt that the only way to secure equal resources was to be educated in the same building with Whites. I hope they did not believe that simply sitting next to a White child, somehow through osmosis, would enhance academic achievement. I'm still wondering how the Clarks thought being educated with Whites would encourage African American youth to choose dolls that looked like them. I have always taken the position that the most important factor affecting academic achievement is not the facilities or who you sit next to, but who is in front of the class! In my opinion, the greatest travesty resulting from *Brown vs. Topeka* is the devastating loss of African American teachers. A study conducted by William Nelson at Ohio State University revealed that of 467 school districts surveyed, 34 had dismissed African American principals, 127 had dismissed African American teachers, 197 had demoted African American principals and 103 had demoted African American teachers.

One example cited was the state of Virginia which

once boasted of having 125 African American high school principals, most of whom had advanced degrees, had dwindled to 13 and falling.[1] Presently, African Americans are 17 percent of the national public school population, but comprise only 8 percent of the teachers, with an exceedingly low 1.2 percent being African American males. Estimates project by the year 2000, African Americans will be 25 percent of the national public school student population and 5 percent of the teachers. African Americans may be the only race expecting someone else to educate their children. I'd like to believe that the leaders and proponents of *Brown vs. Topeka* couldn't have fathomed the virtual elimination of the African American teacher.

According to Bill Moss, school board member from Columbus, Ohio, school districts which are run by corporate interests and unions have abolished the notion of educating children to play a game of "racial numbers." Most unions are adamant about the racial quota of White teachers in predominantly African American schools, but relax the policy in White schools. There are thousands of inner city African American schools with only a staff that is 25 to 40 percent African American. What is wrong with African American children being taught by their role models when numerous research studies conclude that teachers often lower expectations based on the race, income, gender, and appearance of the child?

Please don't misunderstand my contention, I'm not stating that all African American teachers give high expectations for African American students and that White teachers do the same for White students, but desegregation and playing "racial number" games has not been beneficial for African American students.

III

Many White female teachers rather than attempting to educate our youth have placed them in special education classes or have suspended them. I have throughout this introduction carefully chosen to use the word desegregation, not integration. These two words are not synonymous. The former is forced, assumes superiority and places the burden on the victim. The latter is voluntary, provokes mutual respect and the burden, if any, is mutually shared. Integration does not assume that African American schools that produced generations of African American scholars would close, nor result in the demotion of teachers and principals. It also does not assume that a curriculum that once taught Frederick Douglass and Abraham Lincoln, Lewis Latimer and Thomas Edison, Granville Woods and Alexander Bell would now exclude African American leaders, reserving their recognition for the month of February. True integration encompasses a multicultural curriculum.

Schools that look integrated on the outside are highly segregated on the inside. This is clearly evident with tracking and magnet schools. The former allows children to be divided based on IQ and standardized tests. Both have been determined in numerous studies to be culturally biased. A school could possess a 50-50 Black-White population, but administer a 90 percent White advanced placement-honors division and a 90 percent African American basic track. Unfortunately, many African American parents, especially those that don't visit the schools, are unaware of this phenomenon.

The other feature of deception are magnet schools or schools designed to keep the few White students in the city from suburban flight. Many African American children that live across the streets from these schools are bussed across town in deference to these ''committed'' White children that persevered in the city. My experience in Africentricity has taught me that instead of exclusively studying the African American history, you must also study the oppressor. The question I begin to raise is, why did the Nixon administration, Fortune 500, Trilateral Commission, local Chambers of Commerce, and the unions promote the desegregation of schools? I have found that if you follow the money trail, answers will begin to appear. In the city of Boston alone, 12 million dollars annually is spent on bussing 22,000 students from their neighborhood schools. This figure does not include the four million dollars for additional bus drivers, nor the 25 million dollars per year spent for the police to handle persistently violent resistance.

The ruling class has economically taken advantage of racial fears. Real estate developers and agents have sold White homes below market value, sold them at higher prices to the expanding African American community, and built new homes for Whites in the suburbs. Desegregation has been financially rewarding for the bus companies, oil suppliers, banks, lawyers, real estate professionals, insurance companies, and numerous sundries. Over the past four decades, numerous local leaders and community residents have voiced opposition about waking their child at 4:00 in the morning to be bussed 20 miles to a school that will place their child in special education. Because their last names were not Marshall, Clark, Hooks, or Jackson, the national media has not exposed the grass-root dissatisfaction. We must always question leadership that receives financial support from the establishment

V

because their solutions seem to always lead us away from ourselves.

Thank God for sending us Pansye Atkinson and her exemplary book. She raises the Africentric questions about *Brown vs. Topeka* and provides a clear analysis and prescription for empowerment. Pansye and I are both aware that today's Black colleges that receive only 17 percent of African American students produce almost half of the African American graduates. We have already lost colleges such as Tennessee and Kentucky State and may lose colleges in Mississippi and Louisiana in the name of desegregation. Pansye Atkinson encourages us to re-examine the historically effective African American schools and with the help of the late Ron Edmonds' research, we will find that the most salient factor that contributes to the education of African American children is high expectations from principals and teachers that look like them.

Jawanza Kunjufu, Ph.D.

Did our best legal black minds, do the right thing?

ERRATA

Due to a publishing error, the following information was omitted from the beginning of chapter one, A PEOPLE AT RISK.

The publisher regrets this error and it is not to reflect on the integrity or scholarship of the author in any manner.

This writer was puzzled by and curious about--as were innumerable other Americans--frequent and vague print and television editorials in the spring and summer of 1984 about the "tragic" death of a young and successful Chicago African American female journalist. On August 5, 1984, The Washington Post ran an article which made clear to this writer subtleties about which many editorials had only hinted when it detailed the "generic" suicide in May of Leanita McClain "who lost her way" at the "racial frontier." The article highlighted the plight that the suicide reflected: "A suicide by a Black female is an extraordinarily rare event in America (2.4 per hundred thousand, contrasted with 6.0, 12.2, and 20 for White females, Black males, and White males respectively), according to the National Center for Health Statistics." Although she had other personal problems, McClain, a "rising star," seemed despondent over racial struggles. She was particularly disturbed by the conflagration ignited by the 1982-83 Chicago Black-White mayoral race --which apparently opened her eyes to some realities of race relations--and became perplexed by her own racial identity in the context of her professional world. California specialist Richard Seiden was quoted: "A steady increase (in suicide) is inevitable as Blacks move away from their roots and enter the white professional world" (Klose, C2). But, Leanita McClain represents only one facet of the contemporary African sojourn in America. There is the ongoing drama of a young Los Angeles, unemployed, African American male construction worker named King--Rodney G. King--with a criminal record (Duffy, et al., 24) reported in virtually every media source since early 1991. The brutal beating of inebriated, 25-year-old Rodney G. King--who had led police on a high-speed chase--by four White police officers was unique in Los Angeles only in that it was captured on video tape and submitted to the media by an amateur who happened to be nearby at the time of the March 3, 1991, midnight-hour occurrence. The video tape has been aired on national television numerous times, so Americans are painfully aware of the details of the 81-second (Cohn & Kaplan, 36-37) brutality. Though morbid was the beating with nightsticks by the four police officers, the revelation by the media that as many as 14 officers stood by and watched is frightening to contemplate.

But for the video tape, the four responsible police officers might never have been brought to trial on a charge of excessive force in the arrest of King. On April 29, 1992, millions of Americans were stunned by "not guilty" verdicts rendered by a jury of ten Whites, one Asian, and one Hispanic in Simi Valley, California--the defense was granted this change of venue for the trial (Mathews, et al., 33). Although at least two representative national polls indicated that no more than 5 to 12 percent of Whites agreed with the "not guilty" verdict (The Washington Post May 3, 1992, A26; Newsweek May 11, 1992, 30), the power of institutionalized racism is revealed in that the "system" provided a jury that reflected the minority opinion. Apparently, the jury chose "sides" rather than choosing to "do the right thing."

The excuse of the officers for the beating was that King posed a serious threat and refused to succumb. But, 1) the video tape seems to clearly show that after a point, the almost continued movement of King's body was due to spontaneous bodily reaction to the blows of the nightsticks; and 2) the taped, gleeful voices and dehumanizing remarks of the police officers as they relayed the fact of the arrest to headquarters gave no indication of fear of the victim but, rather, indicated that they enjoyed this and past brutalities. Not surprisingly, the brutality of police in Los Angeles and other American cities to African Americans, and other minorities, has not gone unnoticed by the rest of the world. Soon after the April 29, 1992 verdict and the consequent riots or, more properly, uprisings which immediately followed in South Central Los Angeles and several other locations in the country, Amnesty International, an organization which monitors human rights abuses around the world, cited the Los Angeles Department and sheriff's office for targeting minorities for the use of excessive force and police dog attacks (CNN News, June 6, 1992).

For the writer, the Rodney G. King phenomenon evokes thoughts of assassinated civil rights leader Reverend Martin Luther King, Jr., and seems a prophetic indication that time is running out for the

healing of the American society. The name "King" has come full circle--from the pulpit to the prison--to symbolize African American oppression. At the same time--the name seems a dual omen, with clear, though perhaps disparate, messages to the oppressor and the oppressed. Although the prosecutors chose not to put King on the witness stand during the trial of the four police officers, astonishingly to some, he went before America via television during the rioting/uprisings with an impassioned plea for peace, entreating in a quivering voice, "can we all get along?" and announcing that "we just gotta" (Mathews, et al., 30).

Rodney G. King is representative of the one in four African American males between the ages of 20 and 29 that the 1990 Sentencing Project study (Mauer) found is either imprisoned or under some form of criminal jurisdiction. The same report further indicates that, during the course of a year, more---- than one in four African American males would be processed by the criminal justice system. The study concludes that there are more young African American males "under the control of the criminal justice system" than the total number of African American males of all ages enrolled in college"--609,690 vs. 340,000 as of 1986 (in the "Congressional Black Caucus Higher Education Braintrust Fact Sheet"--1990). Even if the statistics were exaggerated, general knowledge substantiates need for concern.

Insert the following text in Chapter two, page 12 at the end of the second paragraph.

Each one serves as a symbol of the "equal opportunity" that exists for all who would only partake of it, which further alienates the masses of their race. Those who have achieved limited privilege with their new status often either wittingly or unwittingly act in the capacity of indirect rule for the colonizers. Many teachers and other professionals, for example, contribute to the cycle of psychological occupation, deracination, and dehumanization of themselves and other African Americans as they emulate the colonizer's values and foster colonial purposes. Moreover, as Edna Bonacich points out, many middle-class African Americans "partake of the highly ideological, self-deluding myth of capitalism: that the pursuit of individualistic advancement into the middle class will produce social benefit," and that the "benefits of competition will trickle down to everyone.'' And some who have the intent to benefit their communities find that ''institutional impediments'' which require commitment to maintaining the status quo negate that possibility (1988, 86). Perhaps more than any other segment of African American society, middle-class and more affluent African Americans exhibit the characteristics of the psychologically occupied.

It may be argued that African Americans have existed as neocolonial subjects since the end of slavery. But, some theorists, like Robert Staples and the early Robert Allen, have applied that term to the Contemporary African American condition, given the benefits of civil rights measures of the 1950's and 1960's, including the Brown decision; the Civil Rights Act of 1964; the 1965 Executive Order 11246, which enacted Affirmative Action; the Voting Rights Act of 1965 and the Fair Housing Act of 1968. Central to this context is the American economic system of capitalism, which has even more significantly impacted upon African Americans under neocolonialism, as a few have been allowed into the ranks of the corporate elite, and/or have bought into capitalist values. Capitalism--with its classism component, which holds some at the bottom of the economic ladder so that a privileged few may remain at the top--as well as racism, serves colonialism/neocolonialism well. Moreover, it is submitted that capitalism, classisms, racism, and colonialism all support a corporate culture, while exploiting the African American colonized.

1

A PEOPLE AT RISK

PSYCHOLOGICAL OCCUPATION

It has become increasingly apparent to the writer, and to some other African American educators in elementary, secondary, and post-secondary institutions of education, that the escalation of direct control of African Americans by the dominant society in these and other institutions of socialization has a direct relationship to such examples as presented above. In the latter half of this century, countless numbers of Black/African American students, in search of equality, have either wittingly or unwittingly admitted to being unequal to the dominant society by 1) becoming even more like Frantz Fanon's *Black Skin, White Masks* (1967) than prior generations--sometimes capable (although too often equipped with an armor-like facade of self-confidence and accomplishment), but often times confused and perverted by a distaste for or bent on destroying their own kind; or 2) accepting the responsibility for their lack of educational accomplishment and for their consignment to the burgeoning "dungheap" of the dominant society's cast(e) offs--

the essential sacrificial souls of America, Incorporated. All told, Black educational accomplishment, self-knowledge, self-love, and the sense of Black community--physical and spiritual-- are in a constant state of degeneration.

Although the older generations have not been unaffected, for the past several decades, African American youth have been the primary victims of deracination and dehumanization imposed by White America. Young African Americans are required increasingly to function within the context of the value system of the dominant society, although their background experience and/or their inherited history and value system have not prepared them to adequately understand the dominant value system, let alone to affect the delicate balancing of conflicting values essential to Black individual and collective well-being. Many African American youths--lacking the foundation of cultural and racial identity afforded most African Americans of earlier generations--appear to be victims of a type of non-surgical lobotomy, intended to fashion them for the tolerance of the dominant society. Or, they are often rendered ''lost'' within their own culture and rejected by the dominant culture.

This is a strong accusation, but one that is founded in part upon situations which the writer, a former public school teacher, witnessed in a metropolitan school system--situations in which the practices and policies of some non-Black administrators and teachers in control contributed to the programming of young African American heads and hearts for failure and actual dehumanization. Sadly, African American children who did not escape this kind of treatment are in no position as adults to do much about assuring a better life for their children. Moreover, many African American children who escaped academic failure often did not have adequate nurturance in school, or role models who would help them to resist dehumanizing forces. Consequently, as adults and teachers today, as well as parents, they contribute to the perpetuation of oppression and dehumanization of other African Americans. The above exposition defines but the tip of the iceberg of the plight of Black America/African Americans. The writer asserts that:

- There is a preponderance of evidence indicating that the deteriorating condition of Black America is directly related to the advancing state of what will here be termed psychological occupation of Black America by White America and to the consequent deracination and dehumanization of Black America.
- The psychological occupation of Black America by White America is an ongoing phenomenon resulting, in large measure, from the mechanism of cultural repression which permeates the institution of education in the American system of internal colonialism, whereby Black America exists as a domestic colony of White America.
- This state of psychological occupation has been accelerated by the assumptions of the *Brown v. Board of Education of Topeka* Supreme Court Decision of 1954 and its interpretation/implementation.

This discourse suggests that the above thesis mandates that Black America galvanize its forces to reclaim its institutions to audaciously create the political authority to intervene--with the intensity of the physical intervention during slavery of the Underground Railroad movement--in the disastrous fact of the reinforced assault on the Black/African American psyche and the consequent impact on the precious commodities of Black/African American community and unity.

The internal colonialism concept is controversial among African American scholars, but is well-suited to the writer's assumptions regarding the general psychological condition of African Americans. The term colonialism refers to a system of political control by a state, or country, over a foreign territory. Members of the ''home state'' settle in that territory (Staples 1976, 37), effecting a nexus. Internal colonialism--or domestic colonialism--differs in that the colonized are a part of the same country as the colonizers (Blauner 1969, 393-408 passim; Staples 1976, 37-47 passim).

Further discussion of internal colonialism will follow. But first, to facilitate clarity, an explanation of the terms psychological occupation, cultural repression, deracination, and dehumanization is in order.

Psychological Occupation and Cultural Repression

The writer's term psychological occupation refers to a state in which the collective mind, or psyche, of a people, is under the primary influence of an oppressor, or alien force, which confuses distinctions between that oppressor's interests and those of the victims' kind. Such a state engenders actions which reinforce subjugation, as the victims' minds are used against the victims, themselves. Under a system of internal colonialism, cultural repression, which is effected most significantly through education, is a mechanism which facilitates psychological occupation of the colonized.

4

Cultural repression assaults cultural and historical memory as the colonizer promotes acceptance of the colonizer's culture and history as superior to that of the colonized. The oppressed are mystified and made "ashamed of themselves and their values and their history" (Bennett 1975, 211), and thus suffer from loss of identity and ethos.

The "interiorization" concept of Brazilian educator Paulo Freire, although not specific to the internal colonialism model, is applicable here. Freire submits that an oppressed people actually "interiorize" the culture of a dominant class, rather than merely imitating that culture. Freire states that,

> their apparent imitation of the dominators' models is a result of the interiorization of these models and, above all, of the myths of the superiority of the dominant classes that cause the dominated to feel inferior. What in fact is pure interiorization appears in a naive analysis to be imitation. At bottom, when the dominated classes reproduce the dominators' style of life, it is because the dominators live "within" the dominated. (1985, 53)

Among other of Freire's concepts applicable here is a "domesticating practice of education." Having in the past similarly applied the term "domesticated" to the African American condition, the writer considers this concept with interest. For Freire, a "domesticating practice of education" is in direct opposition to a "liberating practice of education," which allows learners to develop "critical consciousness," which undergirds the struggle to be free of domination (101-102). Education for domestication is "prescriptive" (102) and "strives to 'domesticate' consciousness,

5

transforming it. . . into an empty receptacle," to be filled with the words of the educator (114). Freire posits that the "essential" point of this practice, whether done consciously or unconsciously, is the "manipulative dimension between educators and learners, by which the latter are made passive objects of action by the former" and by which a "false consciousness" is imparted to learners (101-102), negating the learners' capacity for clear perception of reality and, consequently, critical reflection. Freire notes:

In such educational practice, the social structures are never discussed as a problem that needs to be revealed. Quite the contrary, these structures are made obscure by different forms of action that reinforce the learners' "false consciousness." (102) With regard to the condition of the African American psyche, African American scholars/educators have made references similar to the psychological occupation concept. These include, for example, educator/historian Carter G. Woodson's reference to the "Negro's mind" being "brought under the control of the oppressor" (1933, xxxiii), and social historian Lerone Bennett, Jr.'s reference to the colonizer's penetration into the "secret zones of the minds and bodies of victims" (1975, 211). Also, others have applied specific terms to the phenomenon of the control of the minds of oppressed people. Psychologist Na'im Akbar, for example, has used the term "psychological slavery" in his description of the dominant class' manipulation of the African American mind.

Deracination

Deracination, as applied here, results when a people are torn away from the sustaining knowledge of their historical-cultural roots and ethos. Although the colonizer's culture and ethos are imposed in the psychological occupation process, the colonized are essentially rejected by the colonizer. Thus, divorced from their own heritage and rejected by that of the colonizer, the colonized are rendered rootless and are alienated. This deracinated state is a critical component of dehumanization.

Dehumanization

Dehumanization may be characterized by deprivation of a number of human qualities and dignities. The concern here is with dehumanization manifest in the alienation and domination that proceed from psychological occupation. A people psychologically occupied react similarly to animals, whose relationships with the world are non-historical, and who have not the capacity for reflective thinking.

Lacking the capacity to react differently, animals adapt themselves to their circumstances in order to survive (Freire, 70-71). The psychologically occupied respond much in the same manner to an oppressive sociocultural reality, basically oblivious to their potential for modifying that reality, in order to improve their lot, or "to be more" (Freire, 70). Lacking significant critical consciousness, the psychologically occupied have not the capacity for the human dignity inherent in self-determination.

The above explanation of key terms should permit clearer understanding of the remaining sections of this discourse, which explore major factors central to the above thesis.

The psychological occupation of black America by white America is a form of

2

INTERNAL COLONIALISM

COLONIALISM, NEOCOLONIALISM AND CAPITALISM

Some theoreticians argue that true colonialism means domination by a political entity over a people in a foreign territory. However, when one compares the treatment of African Americans with European exploitation of people of color everywhere, close parallels are discovered. In 1968, cultural historian Harold Cruse insisted that "the only factor which differentiates the Negro's status from that of a pure colonial status is that his position is maintained in the home country in close proximity to the dominant racial group" (77). Other theoreticians agree that the factor of territoriality is not the essence of colonialism. The essence is the domination of the institutions of a society; thus, they label the history of Black America as one of internal colonialism.

Lerone Bennett, Jr. aptly defines the status of African Americans as that of a colonized people. He cites five constants that prevail in all forms of colonialism:

Whatever the demographic situation, whatever the ideologies and intentions of the colonizers, the system is characterized by five constants: political control, economic exploitation, cultural repression, racism, and force based on superior scientific technology. Of all these constants, the most important and most pervasive is force. (211)

Within that context, Bennett explains how those factors interact in an internal colonialism situation when he describes it as essentially a "mass relationship of economic exploitation based upon inequality and contempt and perpetuated by force, cultural repression, and the political ideology of racism." Bennett stresses that "it follows from this . . . that internal colonialism is the establishment of a colonial relationship between a developing center and an underdeveloped circumference within the borders of the same country" (209). To be sure, the African American colonial experience is unique. Unlike the colonized in the classical model, Black America shares with the oppressor a common language, religion, and even land of birth/citizenship, and is numerically in the minority. These are significant factors in the struggle for "groupness" among African Americans, a prerequisite to institutional resistance to systemic oppression. Additionally, the American economic system of capitalism--founded upon individualism and materialism--and the integral status-ordering system exacerbate the problem of lack of unity as African Americans accelerate the quest for individualism, material gain, and social status. African American Studies scholar and poet Fred L. Hord points out several advantages of African Americans' use of the paradigm of internal colonialism to make a cultural critique of their unique, yet colonial experience:

9

- It relates the condition of African Americans to the condition of African people globally and, therefore--as Lerone Bennett has noted (a) permits the use of Third World analyses and strategies for decolonization; and (b) highlights the commonality of the condition of African people and the objective basis for their global unity.
- Its focus on racist/capitalist institutional domination helps to demystify the problem areas of Black life, including ''class cleavages'' and what African American sociologist James Turner refers to as ''the rhetoric of the civil rights struggle in which so much progress was based on the hope of interracial harmony and unity.''
- Its focus on the central role of cultural repression in the subjugation of a people correctly suggests that the notion that economics is the most critical factor in Black oppression must be reevaluated.
- Its view of the ''culture of the colonized'' as a ''dynamic element'' rather than as a given and therefore a ''basis of group unity''--as, Hord points out, Pan-Africanists have tended to accept it--''aids in the colonized avoiding a flawed cultural critique of their condition and thus a flawed politics'' (1987/88, 35-36).

The writer finds this final point most critical, particularly since the ''dynamic element'' of the culture of the colonized is constantly in tension with the culture of the colonizer. The world view, which defines the ''survival thrust'' (Joseph Baldwin,1985, 216-222 passim) of White America--the colonizer, is necessarily in direct opposition to that of Black America--the colonized; thus, beliefs, values, behaviors, and objec-

10

tives of the two groups cannot be congruent. For example, the Black tendency toward "groupness" and interdependence is based not only on colonized status, but on the African-inherited cosmology. The tension between this cultural quality and that of the colonizer, of atomistic individualism, is of critical import, and this tension has significantly increased since *Brown*. Bennett details succinctly the role of education in internal colonialism as he describes it as a tool of force, asserting that physical force is never enough to contain the colonized:

> But force alone is not enough. In order to create a system, the colonizer must use force to penetrate into the secret zones of the minds and bodies of his victims. And to do that, he relies on several mechanisms, foremost among which is cultural repression, which permeates the whole system, especially the education system, which is used to make the oppressed ashamed of themselves and their values and their history. A point of critical importance here is that the oppressor can use diametrically opposed methods to accomplish the same end. He can forcibly deny the oppressed education, thereby limiting their social and economic possibilities, or he can forcibly "educate" the oppressed, thereby giving them his values and making them instruments of his purposes. Whether he educates or miseducates, whether he uses missionary institutions or mass media, the aim is the same: the planned cultural retardation of a whole people and the systematic repression of their values, insights, and expressions. (211)

Thus detailed, the fact of Black psychological manipulations, exploitation, and oppression would seem undeniable. In such circumstances, the improvement of the Black lot would seem not to be reliant upon Blacks' pulling themselves up by their own bootstraps, but upon their first being freed from a system of education which facilitates and perpetuates the cycle of manipulation, exploitation, and oppression.

As a rule, colonialism relies on collaboration between the colonizer and certain classes among the colonized to assist in stabilizing, or controlling, the colonial community in order to diminish the need for brute force by the colonizer. As Robert Allen has pointed out, neocolonialism (''new'' colonialism) effects a more subtle, indirect means of control through various political, economic, social, or military means, (Allen 1969, 14), after the colonized have been theoretically granted self-determination or emancipation. Self-determination may be an illusion, as the colonizer carefully selects members of the colonized group as ''leaders and authority figures'' who will effect indirect rule for the colonizer (Staples 1970, 41). As an example of such neocolonial dynamics in America, Staples points to Black elected officials who, he states, often hold impressive, but powerless political offices, and who often cater to the values of institutions of the dominator, while ''preaching racial solidarity to the Black masses.'' (41) As important is the fact that African Americans in these and similar positions serve as ''buffers'' for the colonizer, cushioning the relationship between the colonizer and the masses of the colonized.

Hopefully, the reader has recognized from the foregoing general discussion of internal colonialism the reality of the impact of its five constants on African Americans that Lerone Bennett cited. Jonathon Kozol in the book *Savage Inequalities,* documents that some schools within the same states have a $10,000 per-pupil expenditure disparity between their White and African American schools. The focus now turns to the role of education in effecting cultural repression and the escalation of cultural repression and consequent psychological occupation of African Americans that the implementation of the *Brown v. Board of Education of Topeka* Supreme Court Decision engendered.

3

PROPHECIES REVISITED

THE LEGACY OF DESEGREGATION

In addition to the perception of the phenomenon of cultural repression and the role of education in its exercise, it is the assertion of the need for resistance to cultural repression and exploitation through the institutionalization of a collective Black philosophy which prompts the writer to employ the internal colonialism model. The writer believes that comprehension of the logic of this paradigm can facilitate the tackling of major impediments to mobilization for development of a collective philosophy. Those impediments appear to be a lack of adequate understanding by Black America:

- that Black America is, indeed, in the grips of psychological occupation and consequent deracination and dehumanization--perpetrated and perpetuated by White America;
- that there are concrete reasons why White America has effected this condition;
- that there is a concrete means of deciphering how this condition has been effected and perpetuated; and

- that there is, thus, a means for determining what can be done to effect strategies for relief from the mechanisms (primarily cultural repression) which effect the oppressive phenomena of psychological occupation, deracination, and dehumanization.

Most critically, the internal colonialism model exposes the central role of the educational institution in the total process of this subjugation of Black America.The deracination/dehumanization phenomenon was predicted by some astute Black educators upon the "victory" of *Brown v. Board of Education of Topeka*, litigated by National Association for the Advancement of Colored People (NAACP) Legal Defense Fund (LDF) attorneys. The first Black president of traditionally-Black Fisk University, sociologist Charles S. Johnson, for example, warned at that time that integration of public education which *Brown* mandated would be implemented vis-`a-vis "anachronistic holdovers of the long abandoned theories of the early part of the twentieth century in the racial attitudes of many of the older white teachers that will probably never be fully corrected before their retirement" (Haney 1978, 94). These attitudes still exist in some situations; but even more pernicious, though subtle, racial attitudes have developed and Black children continue to be pathetically affected.

Equally as prophetic was the reaction of one of the early leaders of the NAACP (Jaynes & Williams eds., 183)--W.E.B. DuBois--eighty-six years of age when the "separate but equal" doctrine was replaced by *Brown*. Derrick Bell--an NAACP Legal Defense and Education Fund attorney in the 1960s--notes that DuBois "predicted accurately as later events were to prove, that school desegregation would mean the dismissal of thousands of Black teachers ... [and] the decline and loss of black culture in desegregated schools. To avoid this loss, DuBois urged that black history be taught at home" (1979, 10). The wisdom of such prophecies is now borne out in the proliferation of reports and studies. For example, the 1984 report *Saving the African American Child,* by the National Alliance of Black School Educators (NABSE), refers to a 1972 assessment of the contemporary condition of Black school children by the National Education Association and to a 1973 indictment by the Southern Regional Council:

> Early in May 1972 the National Education Association reported that "thousands of Black students were being pushed out of school, suspended, harassed, arrested, and in a few instances, killed or maimed." "In addition, the Southern Regional Council reported in November 1973 that African American students had been excluded from extra-curricular activities, tracked into segregated classes, and confronted with condescension or hostility. This dropout picture has not improved much in the past decade. The teacher employment problem remains. There are new means for setting up tracks, such as 'minimal competency testing.' " (20)

Moreover, as the title of the report suggests, the NABSE document is concerned with the "cultural" condition as well as with the academic condition of African American youth. Indeed, the report asserts that "Academic excellence cannot be reached without cultural excellence" (23) and outlines criteria for the measurement of achievement in both areas, emphasizing the need for "truth" in the curriculum for all students.

The NABSE report also notes that many Black public school teachers and administrators in the South have been displaced during "the past decades" (18). The disastrous consequences of this displacement are not only personal but broadly social. Of the utmost significance is the banishment of many Black males from positions of educational leadership and the apparent negative affect on school-age Black males.

Several factors compound the consequences of *Brown*, two of which will be cited here. First, closely related to the *Brown* phenomenon is the 1973 *Adams v. Richardson* ruling by the U.S. District Court for the District of Columbia. The *Adams* litigation focused on public higher education and was initiated by the NAACP Legal Defense Fund (LDF). The LDF charged that the United States Department of Health, Education and Welfare (HEW) was failing to take necessary action (by cutting off funds) in ten states under its surveillance to enforce compliance with Title VI of the Civil Rights Act of 1964 which prohibits discrimination on the basis of race, color, or national origin in agencies receiving federal financial assistance. The litigation resulted in another victory for the NAACP.

The *Adams* decision ordered HEW (which has since become the Department of Education) to take enforcement action against the ten states which had been notified by HEW's Office for Civil Rights (OCR) in 1969 and 1970 that they were continuing to operate a dual system of public higher education--one Black, one White. OCR appealed the Adams order to take "enforcement" action and an appeals court effected modification which allowed OCR to require the ten states to develop five-year desegregation plans for evaluation (Mohr, 1977, 1-2). In 1980, eight other states were issued this requirement. The decision is constantly under review. In the summer of 1990, the court ruled the LDF suit invalid and dismissed the case (Jaschik 1990, A1, 22). But the early actions by the court and OCR greatly accelerated the racial integration of higher education. Desegregation plans in all of these states, in various stages of implementation or progress, were still in effect by the early 80s (Jaschik) and the number of Black students entering predominantly White colleges/universities had increased dramatically (Weinberg 1983, 306; Fleming 1984, 162).

Since there has been no generally significant enrollment of Whites in traditionally Black colleges/universities, they have been threatened by decreased enrollments and financial hardships. However, in some instances, increasing White enrollments have transformed traditionally Black institutions into predominantly White institutions, e.g., Bluefield State College (Weinberg 1983, 312), West Virginia State and Lincoln University at Missouri (Berry and Blassingame 1982, 294). The *Ayers vs. Mabus* case (the Mississippi Higher Education Desegregation Case) will have even greater implications in the stability of Black colleges.

In *The Search for Quality Integrated Education*, Weinberg noted the general decline in enrollment of African Americans in Southern traditionally Black colleges from 100 percent in 1952 to 40 percent in 1978 (1983, 272). In a significant study on outcomes for African American students in predominantly White institutions (*Blacks in College*, 1984), psychologist Jacqueline Fleming reported between 60 and 75 percent of Black students enrolled in predominantly White colleges--with one-half of all Black students in two-year colleges (10). Carter and Wilson (1991, 12) reported that in 1990, African American enrollment in African American institutions represented only 17 percent of such students enrolled in higher education. However, Fleming and others, e.g., the Southern Educational Foundation (45), have reported that traditionally Black colleges have been "more effective" in producing Black graduates than have traditionally White colleges (191, 194), and data have indicated that "more than one-half of all bachelor's degrees earned by black students" are from predominantly Black institutions (Jaynes & Williams eds. 178). During the latter part of the 1980s, a trend for Black students to enroll in Black institutions has been noted by researchers. Enrollment by Black students in these institutions increased by 7.6 percent between 1988 and 1990, and by twice that amount between 1986 and 1988 (Carter & Wilson, 11-12).The problem of retention of African American students in predominantly White institutions has been the focus of a number of African American researchers. *The Preliminary Report: Winter 1981 Study of Black Undergraduate Students Attending Predominantly White State-Support Universities* (Allen, Daughtry, & Wilson, 1982), points out that although African American students in any institution of higher education bear significant responsibility for their scholastic and social development, the institution bears the "pivotal role." The report also notes the particular responsibility of state-supported institutions for the education of a diverse population. In the effort to "identify factors and formulate strategies helpful in improving the educational experiences and outcomes of Black students in higher education," the study sought Black student input regarding new policies or programs which would "deal with the problems Black students experience at

19

White universities'' (10-11). The preliminary report cited the following as typical of what students called for:

"A policy to eliminate the ongoing conspiracy to undermine and eventually destroy Black/Minority support services; increase, not reduce, financial aid; implement an effective system of dealing with racist instructors; sponsor and encourage more Black relevant social functions; increase effectiveness and support of Black/Minority support organizations, consortium programs.''(11)

Later reports (1984) from this same study indicated that 65 percent and 73 percent of African American undergraduate and graduate students, respectively, reported incidents of discrimination, sometimes explicit in treatment by college/university employees; for example, patronizing or derogatory remarks by faculty members; excessive requests for identification at various on-campus events; racist symbols, epithets, or mimicry by White students--the most frequently reported (Jaynes & Williams eds., 364-65).

Most significantly, acts of discrimination, racial tension and even violence and aggression have escalated on college campuses since the late 1970s. More than 70 campuses were estimated by the National Institute Against Prejudice and Violence to have experienced "significant racial or ethnic violence in 1987" (Jaynes & Williams eds., 365). A recent example of grand scale confrontations and tensions is at Olivet College (Olivet, Michigan), where more than 35 of 50 African American (total enrollment, 650) students withdrew in spring 1992 because of fear of being attacked--not only by White students, but by klansmen, who were rumored as seen on

20

campus. *Black Issues in Higher Education* reported that difficulties began, according to police, over an argument between a white couple. When the boyfriend and two Black students returned to the young woman's door, she called a white fraternity for help. They confronted only the two Blacks, and eventually, others got involved...(April 23, 1992, 3)

Students who withdrew were given permission to complete classes by mail. And in the wake of the widely-publicized "brawl," Olivet's president resigned (*The Chronicle of Higher Education,* May 13, 1992, A4).

Given the many problems that these African American students on White campuses face, individually and collectively, often without credible support, it is understandable that Fleming's research indicated that they most often suffer assault upon their psyches (189).

Second, compounding Black America's integration problem is the instability of certain social institutions of the dominant culture. For African Americans, increased racial integration in all of society's social systems--a natural extension of *Brown* and *Adams*--has resulted in the accrual of the integrator's intellectual and social faux pas along with the integrator's cultural tenets.

Particular concern has been expressed about the institution of education, as in The National Commission on Excellence in Education's *A Nation at Risk* (1983). Citing education as the institution which "undergirds American prosperity, security, and civility," the Commission's report stated that the "educational foundations of our society are presently being eroded by a rising tide of mediocrity that threatens our very future as a Nation and as a people." So severe is the problem, it submits, that "if an unfriendly foreign power had attempted to impose on America the medio-

21

cre educational performance that exists today, we might well have viewed it as an act of war'' (5). The family is another institution in a state of decline in the society at large. In both the education and the family institutions, many of the traditional African American strengths have been replaced or diluted by the trickle-down values of the dominant society which do not undergird an essential African American "survival thrust." An early resource on African American family strengths is Robert Hill's *The Strengths of Black Families* (1971), which details the characteristics contributing to African Americans' strong kinship bonds; strong work orientation; adaptability; and strong religious orientation. African Americans must be mindful of such traditional strengths and resist the attempts by the dominant society to place the blame for decadence on their increased integration into the dominant society's institutions.

The NAACP and Legal Defense Fund

Let it be understood that it is with high regard for the committed professionals of the National Association for Colored People and the Legal Defense Fund that the writer submits in this work criticism of the *Brown* litigation. It is offered also with the realization that we African Americans fight on different levels to overcome inequality and injustice, most often being required to gain in one hand what might in the end need to be traded for a better gain in the other.

The NAACP is the nation's oldest civil rights organization. Founded in 1909 as an interracial organization, the NAACP evolved from the 1905 "Niagara Movement" initiated by Black intellectuals and social activists, including the distinguished scholar-activist W.E.B. DuBois. The Legal Defense Fund, Inc., which handles NAACP litigation, was organized in 1939, but became independent of its "parent organization" in 1955 (Jaynes & Williams Eds. 183-84).

The organization has undertaken litigation of many civil rights efforts from the 1940s to the present, including litigation of *Brown v. the Board of Education of Topeka* in 1952 (Kluger 1977, 540). Without the leadership and litigation efforts of the NAACP and LDF, it is difficult to imagine what would have been the state of race relations and civil rights in twentieth-century America. LDF litigation efforts have persisted since its beginnings, peaking in 1970. These efforts continue, with school desegregation and employment discrimination issues as primary concerns during the past four decades (Jaynes & Williams Eds., 184-85). Much of the contemporary criticism, both internal and external to the NAACP often seems to lose sight of the significance of the contributions of that organization. Dedicated and brilliant attorneys of the NAACP/LDF have given what amounts to life's blood to numerous civil rights battles in the nation's courts.

No one gave more than Thurgood Marshall, an early chief counsel with the LDF, who was to be appointed by President Lyndon B. Johnson in 1967 as the first Black Supreme Court Justice (NAACP 1982, 18), and who served brilliantly until his retirement in 1991. By the time of *Brown*, Marshall had been in "fifteen previous Supreme Court cases, either as chief counsel making the oral argument or with a decisive hand in fashioning the brief, and won thirteen times" (Kluger, 561).

Marshall is reported as having expressed his fatigue and weariness during the extensive litigation travel of the five desegregation cases which were to be finally argued before the Supreme Court in *Brown*. In one

Marshall commented "how tiresome it was trying to save the white man's soul."

instance (1951), Marshall indicated to a colleague how tiresome it was "trying to save the white man's soul" (Kluger, 324). As *Brown* litigation before the Supreme Court approached in 1952, Marshall's wife noted how he had aged over a five-year period and that he had become a "nervous" individual. She reflected upon the toll that the "discouraging job" he had "set" for himself had taken. Longtime friend and advisor William Hastie has since added that, "he drove himself to and beyond the limits of the human anatomy. He was at a point of exhaustion in trying to dispel the sense of defeatism that had inflicted itself on so much of black America" (Kluger, 561). *A Common Destiny* (Jaynes & Williams eds.) reports that:

> At the national level, the NAACP reached its peak influence during the years bracketed by the *Brown* school desegregation decision of 1954 and the passage of the Voting Rights Act in 1965. It had the reputation during that period of being the black organization with the greatest influence in Congress and in national politics generally. (184)

The NAACP still remains, *A Common Destiny* states, the "premier black organization" in terms of membership (450,000 in the late 1970s) and reputation, although there now exist a variety of specialized organizations devoted to social and economic development in the black community (184).

The Logic of *Brown*

For the dominant society, the overriding objective in race relations has been the establishment and perpetuation of White supremacy as justification for political, economic, and social subjugation and exploitation

24

of Black America. The dominant society has been faced with the ever-present need for the improvement of its world image and for the maintenance of the status quo within the context of changing national and international economic and social conditions. Such motivation required the progression from the 17th century institution of slavery to the 1857 *Dred Scott* declaration that Blacks were, "beings of an inferior order... and had no rights which the white man was bound to respect"; to the Emancipation Proclamation (1863); to the *Plessy v. Ferguson* relegation of Blacks by Whites to "separate but equal" facilities and social institutions (1896); to the language of *Brown,* which avoided directly overturning the pronouncements of either *Dred Scott* or *Plessy* (this assertion will be discussed subsequently).

Looking back, *Brown* appears to have served an immediate need of White society to display an act of morality before the world at a critical time in American history (post-World War II era)--a time when America wished to secure itself as a democratic leader of the free world, to pacify the growing unrest in the Black community in its quest for equality, and to invalidate, and ultimately nullify, not only that quest but Black consciousness and Black community, per se. Greater access to the credentials of education created a larger Black middle-class buffer to help quell the discontent of the lower Black ranks. Upward mobility for some, vis-a-vis the seemingly permanent consignment of many to the bottom of the barrel has, sadly, reinforced class consciousness among African Americans, to their detriment. A legal instrument was necessary in the pursuit of racial equality in education and for the demise of Jim Crowism. However, in retrospect, it is clear that not only the interpretation and implementation of *Brown* were destined to heap more detriment on Black America, but that the language of the Supreme Court's much heralded decision reinforced the pattern of American race relations. The irony of ironies is that the language, the interpretation, and the implementation of the *Brown* decision were influenced and sanctioned by Black social-science and NAACP legal experts--victims of cultural repression through education--who were entirely earnest in their efforts and whom Black America, as a whole, supported and rejoiced with upon the "victory" of *Brown.*

An examination of the history of the education of African Americans by White America reflects the use of "diametrically opposed methods", which Bennett cites, effected appropriately as the system of cultural repression has been refined throughout the developing system of American "democracy."

The treatment of the education of African Americans by Whites in America was, at first, proscribed, to secure what Frederick Douglass termed "irresponsible power" (1973, 35; original publication date: 1845), while preventing the "power of truth" (42). Teaching the slave to read and, thus, to learn, would--according to one of Douglass' masters--"ever unfit him to be a slave. He would at once become unmanageable, and of no value to his master." Instructing a slave in reading, the master warned his wife, was both "unlawful," as well as "unsafe" (36). After emancipation of the slaves, education was prescribed, through the Christian/classical vocational curricular emphases, and often filtered through African American instructors in segregated schools and colleges. Carter G. Woodson, of course, scorned such education of African Ameri-

26

cans in his early twentieth century *Miseducation of the Negro* (1933).

Under *Brown,* particularly *Brown* II which in 1955 mandated integration with "all deliberate speed," prescription was reinforced, facilitated by direct, controlled doses. And then, the 80s ushered in a swing of the pendulum, which actually began in the late 70s, resulting in declining education, employment, and other social equalities for African Americans. This was aided by other hardly accidental negative political and social ambiences which effected proscription. Black America, beset on one side by prescription and on the other by proscription, entered the 1990s between the proverbial rock and a hard place. The writer asserts that this vice-like condition is central to the appalling condition of Black America within the system of internal colonialism.

It is important to remember that the condition of internal colonialism was not dismantled when *Brown* declared illegal the forced segregation of the Black and White races in public schools, nor has any court ruling or law passed since *Brown* disrupted the condition of African Americans as a colonized people. Moreover, the irony of *Brown* is that the internal colonialism mechanism of cultural repression was reinforced through more manipulative prescription than in the past, for its advent was cloaked in the rhetoric of "integration" as "equality." The re-establishment of more direct control was not generally anticipated by Blacks since the rhetoric of the *Brown* decision, as well as *Brown* advocates, promised for Blacks their long sought equality.

Educational researcher Asa Grant Hilliard, III has emphasized that the control of the institutions of socialization by oppressors has catastrophic consequences, particularly since this control reinforces cultural repression. After a decade or more of the implementation of *Brown*, Black Americans began to realize the ironies of that "victory" and that the measure of control that they had effected in segregated schools-- a critical degree of self-determination--was in many ways preferable to the almost total lack of control afforded in most integrated education. Vis-`a-vis this dramatically reduced degree of control under mandated integration, disturbing developments in the educational, social, and economic conditions of Black America have been a primary influence in the re-examination of *Brown* by the African American community.

4

OF HINDSIGHT
AND BACKDOORS

CARTER G. WOODSON'S WARNING

Reflection upon the *Brown* phenomenon calls to mind a caveat of historian and educator Carter G. Woodson and prompts the writer to relate that caveat to the internal colonialism mechanism of cultural repression which is forced upon the oppressed in part through prescribed education--formal and informal. In the preface to *Miseducation of the Negro,* Woodson bemoaned:

> No systematic effort toward change has been possible, for taught the same economics, history, philosophy, literature and religion which have established the present code of morals, the Negro's mind has been brought under the control of his oppressor. The problem of holding the Negro down, therefore, is easily solved. When you control a man's thinking you do not have to worry about his actions. You do not have to tell him not to stand here or go yonder. He will find his ''proper place'' and will stay in it. You do not need to send him to the back door. He will go without being told. In fact, if there is no back door,

he will cut one for his special benefit. His education
makes it necessary.(xxxiii)

Review of the hindsight of some *Brown* critics has
led the writer to submit that no matter by what door
entry to *Brown* proceedings occurred for Black
America, Black America unwittingly exited through
the ''back door.'' White America aided Black America
in cutting that door during the *Brown* proceedings. In
this section of discourse, the writer frames several
scholarly analyses of *Brown* which support this line of
reasoning.

Such analyses notwithstanding, it is well to first
note that primary early responses to the dangers of
Brown were those of the Black Power and Black
Nationalist advocates of the 60s. Central to the thrust
of these groups was ardent criticism of the miseducation
of Blacks and, thus, Black cultural crisis--exacerbated
by the *Brown* mandate. The Student Nonviolent Coor-
dinating Committee (SNCC), Us Organization, the
Congress of Racial Equality (CORE), and the Black
Panthers were key organizations which not only regis-
tered criticism and protest, but took concrete action to
foster self-determination for African Americans in economic, political, and educational realms. Such groups
took steps to effect implementation of increased control of school policy by Blacks in their communities as
well as alternative educational institutions. In predominantly White institutions of higher education, the
Black Power and Black Nationalist movement pro-
moted the implementation of Black Studies and Black
student cultural/political organizations. Although Black
America achieved major gains during the thrust of the
60s, the 70s ushered in a decline of this influence of

Black self-determination (Karenga 1982, 133-134). The consequences of this decline have no doubt prompted increasing scholarly critiques of *Brown*, some of which will be reviewed here.

Before focusing the discussion on some significant scholarly analyses of *Brown*, it will be useful to recount the five constants of all forms of colonialism as noted by Lerone Bennett, to facilitate the reader's focus on the centrality of the internal colonialism paradigm to the writer's thesis. These constants are:

- political control;
- economic exploitation;
- cultural repression,
- racism; and
- force--based upon superior scientific technology.

Bennett cites force--physical and psychological--as the most critical and pervasive element. Moreover, in internal colonialism, he details cultural repression as the foremost mechanism of force, used most effectively through the education system to effect "the planned cultural retardation of a whole people and the systematic repression of their values, insights, and expressions."

These mechanisms of internal colonialism appear even more devastating to Black America since the implementation of the mandated "mixing" and, frequently, "balancing" of the races in public schools and later in post secondary education which followed the *Brown* decision. Whether or not the Supreme Court *Brown* opinion and/or the desegregation implementation strategy were "planned" to effect the "cultural retardation" of Black America and the "systematic repression of their values, insights, and expressions," this is the ever-evolving reality of the post-*Brown* era.

Representative Black professionals who have during the 1970s and early 1980s or so documented their interpretations that the *Brown* victory has proven merely an instrument for the perpetuation of the cycle of White domination of African Americans are Donald L. Howie of the Yale University Law School (in 1973); Derrick Bell, a civil rights lawyer of the 60s and early 70s, for a while with the NAACP Legal Defense and Educational Fund, of the Harvard Law School (in 1979, 1980); Robert L. Carter, a former NAACP *Brown* attorney, and a federal district judge in New York (in 1980); and Robert G. Newby, professor of sociology, Wayne State University (in 1979). In *Shades of Black* (1991), psychologist William E. Cross offers some significant observations about the dominant assumption of Black ''self-hate,'' which was a key factor in the *Brown* decision.

Bearing in mind the mechanisms of the internal colonialism paradigm, a review of some central criticisms of *Brown* by these scholars is instructive. Besides criticism of the language and interpretation/implementation of *Brown*, questions are raised by these analysts about some perceived underlying motives of White America in the *Brown* decision, about the strategy employed by NAACP lawyers, and about realized outcomes for Black America. This overview of some criticism of *Brown* is by no means exhaustive, but is adequate to support the writer's contentions about the problems of Black America that *Brown* has helped to intensify.

Dominant Interests

First, a primary criticism asserts that the *Brown* decision reflects more concern with protecting the

32

image and interests of the dominant American society than with providing equality for Black Americans. This criticism is central to the Howie and Bell resources employed here. In a scathing analysis in *The Journal of Black Studies*, Howie points out that the Court argued that the central issue in *Brown* was "the effect of desegregation itself on public education." He quotes the Court:

We must consider public education in the light of its full development and its present place in American life throughout the Nation. Only in this way can it be determined if segregation in public schools deprives these plaintiffs of the equal protection of the laws (*Brown v. Board of Education*, 1954). (Cited in Howie 1973, 375-376) Howie asserts:

> Critical analysis reveals that the Court's argument disguises the perennial socio-legal justification of the denial and constitutional rights of so-called American [sic] citizens. I am specifically alluding to the satanic judicial custom of balancing the precious liberties of Black people over and against the needs and desires of the dominant white culture. The Court's wholly immoral argument implies that if public education were not so essential to American civisme, a state could reasonably maintain a segregated public educational system. Thus the Court invokes a pernicious legacy of Plessy all over again. (379)

Bell's interpretation of the meaning and consequences of *Brown* exhibits skepticism about the motivations of the American System of democracy. He posits:

> "While reliance on law developed under [the] Constitution is the proper refuge of those without alternate political and economic options, it is not

33

now nor has it ever been an appropriate repository of the faith that has brought blacks from bondage to the current societal twilight zone so enthralling to some and so distressing to others'' (1979, 9).

Bell details specific benefits to the dominant culture in the areas of foreign policy, domestic policy, and judicial supremacy. In foreign policy, he asserts that, ''The country's efforts to convince emerging third-world nations to opt for democratic rather than communist forms of government were aided greatly by the abandonment of official segregation at home.'' Moreover, he notes that the ''Federal government's amicus briefs... urged resolution of the problem of racial discrimination within the context of the present world struggle between freedom and tyranny.'' Coverage of the *Brown* decision by the news media, Bell states, ''speculated broadly on its impact on U.S. foreign policy efforts.'' W.E.B. DuBois, he further points out, noted that the *Brown* decision ''would not have been possible without the world pressure of communism'' (10).

In the area of domestic matters, one of the benefits that Bell points out is that the country could ''have its cake and eat it, too,'' in that blacks would remain exploitable economically and a continuing, if misleading reminder to lower-class whites that their status in the society was not, after all, so bad (11-12). Judicial supremacy was enhanced, Bell suggests, by *Brown*:

The enforcement of *Brown*, the task of paramount importance to blacks, was subsumed to a matter of far more concern to the Court and the country. Blatant disobedience to federal court orders was viewed as a

34

threat to the role of the courts and thus to the nation's basic governmental structure. . . . It is now apparent that many decisions favoring school cases handed down during this period were oriented toward countering defiance of the *Brown* ruling, and only coincidentally in obtaining compliance with it. (13) In a subsequent essay in the notable *Shades of Brown* (1980), which he edited, Bell points out that prior to *Brown*, Blacks had for 100 years been attacking the policy of segregated public education. He further explores the value of the decision to Whites, "not simply those concerned about the immorality of racial inequality" (96), and submits the "interest-convergence principle" as the dominant influence in the *Brown* decision.

The interest of blacks in achieving racial equality will be accommodated only when it converges with the interests of whites; however, the fourteenth amendment, standing alone, will not authorize a judicial remedy providing effective racial equality for blacks where the remedy sought threatens the superior societal status of middle-and upper-class whites. (95) Acceptance of this principle leads to a logical conclusion:

> It follows that the availability of Fourteenth Amendment protection in racial cases may not actually be determined by the character of harm suffered by blacks or the quantum of liability proved against whites. Racial remedies may instead be the outward manifestations of unspoken and perhaps subconscious judicial conclusions that the remedies, if granted, will secure, advance, or at least not harm societal interests deemed important by middle and upper-class whites. Racial justice--or its appearance--may, from time to time, be counted among the interests deemed important by the courts and by society's policy makers. (95)

35

A panorama of precedents lends credence to Bell's interest-convergence principle and suggests that this principle informed the language of *Brown*. It is the criticism of that language by the analysts employed in this discussion that is next reviewed here.

The "Language of Inferiorization" (Fanon 1969, 40)

This second criticism insists that the language and/or interpretation which suggests that the separation of Black children from White children in public education necessarily damages Black children psychologically and impedes their ability to learn is a reflection of the low esteem in which Black Americans are held: Black is inherently inferior and dependent upon the White presence for psychological and intellectual development and stability. This language, of course, also serves to protect the image and self-esteem, albeit, the "status" of the dominant society vis-`a-vis the traditional low status of African Americans. The fact that the use of the language and the implementation were influenced by the strategy which the NAACP lawyers for the plaintiffs forged--a strategy which, paradoxically, won the battle but was destined to lose the war-- elicits criticism, and on the part of at least one NAACP *Brown* lawyer, in retrospect, some regret.

First, Newby (1979) submits that *Brown* "was the correct decision for many of the wrong reasons. It is this contradiction which brings us to the possible dilemma of 'integration' being racist." The Court's pivotal statement declared, Howie notes:

> To separate them (black children) from others of similar age and qualifications solely because of their race generates a feeling of inferiority as to their status in the community that may affect their hearts

36

and minds in a way unlikely to ever be undone (*Brown v. Board of Education*, 1950). (17)

Such separation, Newby observes, denotes inferior status of the segregated group; thus, the "primary issue" was that of the status of Blacks as a group. Newby continues:

> The court was not saying and should not have been interpreted as saying, that whenever blacks were separated from whites, blacks were likely to suffer psychological damage. If that were so, well over 95% of Afro-Americans would be in trouble just being at home. Such a contention would be absurd. Nevertheless, the continuing desegregation efforts are designed ostensibly to save blacks from psychological damage. (17)

Newby seems to be saying that the language of *Brown* has been misinterpreted, thus implementation flawed. However, this writer discerns that Newby has chosen to posit his criticism in this manner rather than pronounce the Court's reasoning as absurd. All of these critics express concern about the social science input and implications in *Brown*. The testimony of Black social psychologist Kenneth B. Clark critically influenced the Court's positive decision, but, some would say, precipitated negative outcomes. Central to Clark's testimony were data from the "doll studies" which he and his psychologist wife Mamie had compiled. Newby provides an account of the tests and the results:

> In these "experiments," black children were more likely to pick a white doll than a colored doll as being "nice, pretty," and "looking like themselves." The other study was a coloring test in which they asked

black children to color a face to "look like themselves" (Coloring Book Style). (18)

Newby charts the results of Northern and Southern Black children on the coloring test which indicate that 80% of the children in the South selected "brown" rather than "white" (15%), or "other color" (5%), to "look like themselves," while only 35% of children from the North selected "brown," 44% "white" and 20% "other color." Newby continues:

> An initial inspection of the table suggests that the Southern children's "identity thing" was more "together." But not according to Clark's testimony before the court. Clark explained that while the Southern child "may appear" to be more healthy, his "apparent emotional stability . . . may be indicative only of the fact that through rigid racial segregation and isolation has he accepted as normal the fact of his inferior status". In short, according to Clark's interpretation, black children in the North suffered from low self-esteem as indicated by their (64%) perceiving themselves to be white or some other color. But, black children in the South suffer from low self-esteem because they (80%) perceive themselves to be brown. (19)

And thus, the Court concluded that the separation of Black children from Whites generates a "feeling of inferiority" in Black children! In *Shades of Black* (1991), Cross submits that what the NAACP needed, as Marshall had detailed, was clear-cut evidence that damage was being done to Negro children in segregated schools, just as damage to clients is proved in any other case, and the Clarks' interpretation of the doll-studies data provided that (37-38). The interpretation rendered a "pejorative" (17) image, Cross states, but that image "provided a sharp tool with which the Warren Court could cut a path toward desegregation." (37) Cross concludes:

> As "evidence of damage," the image served its purpose well. Beyond the courtroom, however, and especially in scholarly works that have appeared since the Court's 1954 decision, the image helped distort Black history and the social scientific analysis of Black life. By continuing to interpret the racial-preference studies with singular rather than contrasting images, the isolated and stark presence of the self-hating Negro became what the Clarks and others never intended: a stereotype. (38)

Although Cross questions the Clarks' interpretation of their doll-studies data, he does not question their ethics, and declares that they would never have contrived evidence (36). Cross' *Shades of Black* details a much-needed exploration of the evolution of the "myth" of Black self-hatred (or low self-esteem or self-concept) as the dominant theme in Black identity, and a brief discussion of that evolution here will assist in clarification of the concept, the Clarks' role in its development, and its introduction in the *Brown* litigation. Cross points to the diversity and complexity of the African American personality which social scientific studies have determined since the early 1970s, and decries the simplistic, one-dimensional approach taken by the socio-psychologists who attempted to define that personality between 1939 and the early 1960s. He notes that the "social scientific literature on Negro identity" written between 1936 and 1967 "reported that self-hatred and group rejection were typical of Black psychological functioning" (ix). The Clarks, he points out, are often credited with a "novel theoretical

39

perspective and unique methodology in the study of Negro identity,'' but the theory and methodology are clearly linked to the husband and wife team of Eugene and Ruth Horowitz (15).

Eugene Horowitz's research on racial attitudes employed Black and White children in a ''Show Me Test'' that used photographs of Black and White children (7), although he had considered using Black and White dolls (15). In his results, Horowitz did not interpret a preference for another race as a lack of mental health (7). Ruth Horowitz's 1939 study used a variation of Eugene Horowitz's racial attitudes study to measure racial identity (8) and did interpret Black preschool-children's preference for White identity to indicate a lack of mental health. Cross asserts that Ruth Horowitz, using some truths, half-truths, and exaggerations, worked her way to her ''now-famous interpretation'' that Negro children exhibit ''wishful thinking'' in a preference for White identity (8-10 passim). Ruth Horowitz's study, Cross states, is recognized as the ''first modern empirical study of racial identity in Black and white children'' (7), and that study ''set the stage for the theoretical and methodological orientation to be embraced by researchers of racial identity from 1939 to the present'' (10).

Cross cites several problems with the studies of both Ruth Horowitz and the Clarks. He notes that they recognized the distinctions as well as the correlation between personal identity (PI) and reference group orientation (RGO), and thus the need for measurement of each in assessing personal identity. Cross explains that personal identity (PI) studies examine ''so-called universal components of behavior'' (43), such as self-esteem and degrees of happiness, anxiety, etc., while

40

reference group orientation (RGO) studies examine those "aspects of the self" that are culture, class, and gender specific"--differences in values, perspectives, group identities, lifestyles, and world views (45). Although Ruth Horowitz and the Clarks measured only RGO (group or racial identity), they discussed both RGO and PI in their findings "as if" both had been assessed, with Ruth Horowitz apparently believing that the correlation between the two domains justified this approach (136). The personal identity trait of self-concept, or self-esteem, in Negro children was defined as "low" through the use of the reference group orientation--or racial identity test (136).

Additionally, Cross asserts, conclusions that self-esteem or self-concept was the "driving force" behind choices that children made in racial identity or racial preference experiments were usually justified by anecdotal "evidence" of personality involvement in the "show me"--activities in the tests. The Clarks collected anecdotal data from children in their study and "clinical observations they made of other children in psychiatric treatment." Ruth Horowitz used observational as well as anecdotal material (14,28). Another distorting factor was that much of the research was conducted with children, but was used to draw conclusions about the racial identity of adults. The studies were, Cross asserts, therefore distorted and the findings invalid.

Close scrutiny reveals, Cross states, that the "Negro" children in both Ruth Horowitz's and the Clarks' studies showed the tendency for Black children to be bicultural rather than mono-cultural, embracing two, and sometimes more than two, cultures, which is an interesting and complex trait, rather than a sign of

41

pathology (119-123 passim). But, Cross states, in the Clarks' studies, children who did not show a clear preference for either Blacks or Whites were characterized as retarded (21). Given the history of African Americans and the necessary survival skills developed in an oppressive environment, the bicultural orientation is not surprising, Cross notes (119-123). He also states that the lack of recognition of the strengths and weaknesses of African Americans, of their psychological and social diversity and complexity, has unintentionally "dehumanized" them, by denying that they have a "variety of ways in which they construct themselves" (Raymond, A10) as all humans do.

Through study of the Clarks' early work, Cross discerns that they were concerned about "poorly designed RGO experiments, such as the one by Ruth Horowitz," fearing that researchers might be misled into assigning identity problems to Negro children (137). But, Cross feels that the work of Abram Kardiner and Lionel Ovesey, set forth in *The Mark of Oppression* (1951), which complied with political "correctness" of the period, sealed the direction of the Clarks' research findings on Black identity. Kardiner and Ovesey, following the lead in Gunnar Myrdal's analysis of Negro life and culture in *An American Dilemma* (1944), and in African American sociologist E. Franklin Frazier's 1939 text on the Negro family (*The Negro Family in America*), tried to establish the fact of the Negro's "idealization of white people and white culture and the concomitant rejection of Negro life and culture" (negative group identity), and the consequent damage to personal identity (PI) (low self-esteem). Kardiner and Ovesey "popularized" low self-esteem and introduced the term "self-hatred"--a term initially introduced by European Jews in attempts to ''explicate the essence of a 'bad' and a 'good' Jewish identity''--into the discussion of Negro identity (30-31). In reference to Clark's *Brown* testimony and his subsequent publication *Prejudice and Your Child* (1955) Cross concludes:

> Unfortunately, the effect of the 1954 Supreme Court desegregation decision was the intellectual canonization of the self-hatred thesis. Although based almost entirely on doll studies with preschool children (i.e., inherently unreliable RGO evidence), and with only one PI study (i.e., the Kardiner and Ovesey [1951] ''self-hatred'' study), Clark's (1955) interpretation that Negroes were typically self-hating--a self-hatred he felt was ''easily'' recognizable in the youngest and oldest Blacks--became dogma, rather than an opinion subject to social scientific inquiry. As dogma, the self-hatred thesis was characterized by gaps in knowledge, blind spots, and, on occasion, intellectual intimidation. (129)

Although Cross recognizes the NAACP's legal strategy as effective in the ''struggle to defrock Jim Crow,'' he bemoans the fact that progress in the study of ''Blackness'' was ''sidetracked'' by that struggle. Without the need for the ''proof of damage'' in the *Brown* litigation, he submits, progress may have been made, and more enlightened research traditions established as early as the 1940s, even though such trends as Freudian psychoanalysis, the inkblot or Rorschach tests, and doll tests were strong influences in that period (129).The basic premise of this discourse requires, further on, a closer look at Kenneth Clark and his influence in *Brown* and subsequently. Presently, there are additional analyses of critics to explore.

43

Further observations by Howie center around the two basic Court statements quoted above. There are "two dimensions, or more accurately . . . two syllogisms" in *Brown*, Howie asserts, "though the Court does not itself suggest a formulation or a methodology for determining precisely how they interact" (373). Howie does not actually outline the two syllogisms, but they might be defined as follows:

Syllogism I:
- Segregated public education is detrimental to American civisme.
- Black public education is segregated.
- Black public education is detrimental to American civisme.

Syllogism II:
- Separation of Black children from White children generates a lasting feeling of inferiority in Black children.
- Segregated public education separates Black children from White children.
- Segregated public education generates a lasting feeling of inferiority in Black children. Howie argues:

> The first syllogism seems to be founded on self-evident sociohistorical propositions about the development and meaning of public education in the framework of the Fourteenth Amendment's requirement of the equal protection of the laws. This side of the Court's argument appears on its face to involve an essentially constitutional construction. However, the second syllogism is basically psychologistic: its conclusion reflects the constitutional translation of or inference from socio-psychological data. . . . The

44

manner in which critics of *Brown* have chosen to relate these two syllogisms has determined the theoretical nature of their attacks upon the Court. (373)

Howie contends that the Court apparently felt that the first syllogism--the "constitutional syllogism" (indicted by Howie as ill-phrased) was not sufficient to overturn *Plessy* (separate but equal). However, the "psychologistic" argument, he states, "posed substantial problems for empirical validation (378)". Moreover,

> Given the thorough going anti-empiricism of the Court, one must conclude that its perspective was culturally and politically determined. It was axiomatic that Niggers could only benefit from integration. Though this classic racist assumption inheres generally in Western culture, the Supreme Court judiciously validated and incorporated this anti-human cosmology into its most honorific condescensions. . . . it updated the wretched slaves/masters configuration. . . . The internal "coherence" and "logic" of *Brown* itself--intrinsically considered--demonstrates the amazing extent to which the Court indulged in racist hyperbole. Dred Scott continues to penetrate the supposedly egalitarian curtain of western democracy. (381-82)

Howie also indicts the following statement by the Court as a "left-handed rejection" of *Plessy* which avoided "an explicit renunciation of the assumption of *Plessy* that segregation laws did not necessarily imply the inferiority of the Black" (377-78).

> Whatever may have been the extent of psychological knowledge at the time of *Plessy v. Ferguson* this finding is amply supported by modern authority. Any language in *Plessy v. Ferguson* contrary to this finding is rejected. (378)

Thus, Howie has asserted that both *Dred Scott* (Blacks had no rights which the White man was bound to respect) and *Plessy v. Ferguson* are alive and well. "*Brown* is quintessential *Plessy*" (383), he posits; moreover--"Integrationist millenialism notwithstanding, *Brown* revives and resurrects the nightmarish apparition of Dred Scott" (384).

NAACP Legal Strategy

Now for a look at NAACP strategy in *Brown* and some very explicit regret as revealed by former NAACP lawyer Robert Carter. Carter, as chief counsel for the plaintiffs in Topeka, argued the "color blind" concept congruent with the historical dissent of Justice John Marshall Harlan in *Plessy v. Ferguson*. Carter submitted that:

> The state has no authority and no power to make any distinction or any classification among its citizenry based upon race and color alone. We think that this has been settled by the Supreme Court of the United States in a long line of cases which hold that in order for a classification to be constitutional it must be based on a real difference.... The Supreme Court has also held in a series of cases that race and ancestry and color are irrelevant differences and cannot form the basis for any legislative action. (Cited in Ravitch 1980, 37).

In *Shades of Brown*, Carter's essay "A Reassessment of *Brown v. Board*" reveals enlightening, pragmatic reflection which deserves some attention here. His summary critique of *Brown* is revealed in his opening statements:

> As I seek to assess the reasons black school children have benefited so little educationally from

46

Brown v. Board of Education (*Brown I* and *Brown II*) and despite its being an almost total fulfillment of the strategy we had devised to reach that historical moment on May 17, 1954, it is clear that what we had won was only an engagement, albeit a critical one, in another phase of a long campaign. These negative comments are addressed to *Brown's* reach as a tool to upgrade the educational offerings accessible for black children. (21)

Carter submits that *Brown* will remain prominent in American jurisprudence because of its radical transformation of race relations in this society, however limited its "impact on the educational community." This judgment notwithstanding, he continues:

We are looking to *Brown*, however, to establish through constitutional doctrine equal educational opportunity for black children in real life. The problem, I now believe, was, at least in part, with our strategy. We were locked into a present that was already past, and the Supreme Court's announcement of May 17, 1954, was designed to restructure an era that was dead as soon as the *Brown* decision became law, although it was to linger on for at least two decades before finally giving up the ghost. (21)

Carter explains that the strategy in *Brown*--focused on basic conditions of segregation and thus the disparity between educational resources for Blacks and Whites in the South--was the same as that employed in previous cases of educational inequality argued by the NAACP: *Sipuel v. University of Oklahoma Law School*--1948; *Sweatt v. Painter*--1950; and *McLaurin v. Oklahoma State Regents*--1950. In *Sipuel* and *Sweatt,* (the first time that the NAACP had utilized such strategy), expert testimony was employed to demonstrate that segregated facilities and the "adverse psychological detriment" inflicted on Blacks in segregated situations could not provide equal educational opportunity (22). *McLaurin* was the first case of pure segregation to be argued in the Supreme Court, Carter notes--involving not separate facilities, but segregation within the same facilities. In the *Brown* case, Carter explains:

> The testimony of our social scientists focused on the impossibility of providing equal educational opportunity in a system where racial separation was mandated by law. Accordingly, the basic postulate of our strategy and theory in *Brown* was that the elimination of enforced segregated education would necessarily result in equal education. And as I read *Brown* I, the United States Supreme Court was clearly of the same view. (22-23)

In retrospect, Carter (who recruited psychologist Kenneth Clark as a part of the research team which provided testimony for *Brown*) states that he would not, if faced with preparing for *Brown* again, seek principally social scientists to "demonstrate the adverse consequences of segregation"; rather, he would seek educators to "formulate a concrete definition of the meaning of equality in education," and he would base his argument "on that definition and seek to persuade the Court that equal education in its constitutional dimensions must, at the very least, conform to the contours of equal education as defined by the educators" (27). However, Carter notes: ". . .those educators who supported us never challenged this view" (23). Moreover, he suggests that "the ineffectiveness of professional educators in specifying the

48

educational package necessary for the black urban underclass to achieve equal educational opportunity has helped cause much of the present confusion and controversy'' (26). Educational policy--e.g., teaching methods, curriculum, financing--he contends, should be the focus of civil rights strategy, rather than integration per se. Carter posits that ''to focus on integration alone is a luxury only the black middle class can afford'' (28).

Carter asserts that it was necessary that *Plessy* be dethroned ''as a national standard,'' as it was by *Brown,* not only to end legal segregation, but to destroy the North's myth that it was ''more advanced and progressive than the South in dealing with the race question'' (23). Carter's reference, of course, is to the absence of the ''Jim Crow'' law of segregation in most Northern states, even though de facto segregation was--and is--prevalent.

In summation, the writer outlines below some specifics concerned with the outcomes of *Brown* as addressed by these scholars which can provide focus on areas for further study:
- Negative Developments
- Alternative Directions
- The Racism Impediment

Negative Developments

1.) Bell aptly points out that ''the color-blind constitution theory,'' through which the Court has indirectly ''reneged'' on *Brown,* ''bars effective racial remedies'' (1979, 13). Moreover, contrary to the convergence of interests which he suggests aided in bringing about the *Brown* decision, Bell indicates perception of a ''substantial and growing divergence in the interests of whites and blacks" which is impeding progress toward fulfilling the mandate of *Brown* (1980, 98).

2.) Howie asserts that history will prove that the early hopeful evaluation of *Brown* by "Negro" leadership. . .

> retarded the movement toward Black self-determination, effectively having functioned as a beguiling strategy of the white ruling classes. Because the Black nation embraced the integrationists' puerile view of *Brown*, the essential task of Black liberation was substantially obscured by the necessity of demystifying the assimilationists' cosmology. (372)

3.) These analysts do recognize that substantial evidence of benefits from integration as "racial balance" has been lacking. Newby points out, for example, that two primary reviews of studies of school desegregation results--"School Desegregation: Outcomes for Children," (St. John 1975), and "School Desegregation: An Evaluation of Predictions Made in *Brown v. Board of Education*" (Stephan--in *Psychology Bulletin*, March 1978) "have shown that little, if any, benefits accrue to black or white students as a result of changes in racial composition of schools" (67). In fact, contrary to the U.S. Commission on Civil Rights "Racial Isolation Report" (1967), which tends to support the "separation/psychological damage model," Newby notes that Stephan's review. . . found some studies where the self-esteem of blacks was higher in predominantly black schools. Even more important, he found no studies where the self-esteem of blacks was higher in racially mixed schools. (23)

Moreover, Newby notes a critical observation by

St. John, who states that "in those areas most crucial to personal development, self-esteem and occupational aspirations, the data seems to suggest that 'integration' might well be detrimental to black children" (20).

4.) Cross points to the far-reaching negative effects of the "self-hating Negro" stereotype which Kenneth Clark's testimony to the Court engendered, as he asserts that not only were Black history and social scientific analysis of Black life distorted; Cross observes that "Negro self-hatred gained a concensus in both the scientific and popular press." By 1960, Cross continues, "many assumed that Negro self-hatred was a thoroughly documented finding" (41). Cross' statement rings true, especially if one contemplates the deluge of programs for "culturally deprived" and "disadvantaged" African Americans that emerged in the 1960s and 1970s which were intended to save them from their own kind. Many African American youths consequently adopted the values, world views, and life styles of new role models, but have found that their status does not permit them to comfortably share these new-found styles, and some outcomes have been devastating: shattered families, children having children, robberies and murders committed for the possession of material "things." And there is now the frantic search by politicians and social scientists for the next means of "saving" the "self-hating" African American. But analyses which search for reasons for the decline in positive "family values" among African Americans since the 1950s typically ignore the fact of a major social change in the early 1950: implementation of the *Brown v. the Board of Education* decision.

51

Alternative Directions

1.) Bell concludes that the integrated school has "many potential values as the Court made clear in 1954, but it is not the sole or even the most likely setting, especially for effectively educating poor, black children" (1980, 15). He is critical of those who still contend that equal education can only be achieved through racial balancing. He counts (in 1979) former chief counsel of the NAACP Legal Defense Fund Thurgood Marshall, who had been since 1967 an Associate Justice of the Supreme Court, (Kluger, 760) among those who have not altered their view vis-`a-vis mounting evidence to the contrary. However, Marshall warned, Bell notes, while the NAACP celebrated immediately after the *Brown* victory, "... we ain't begun to work yet" (1979, 10). Bell writes, in *Shades of Brown:*

> Desegregation remedies that do not integrate may seem a step backward toward the *Plessy* "separate but equal" era. Some black educators, however, see major educational benefits in schools where black children, parents, and teachers can utilize the real cultural strengths of the black community to overcome the many barriers to educational achievement. As Professor Laurence Tribe argued, "Judicial rejection of the 'separate but equal' talisman seems to have been accompanied by a potentially troublesome lack of sympathy for racial separateness as a possible expression of group solidarity". (101)

2.) On this topic, Carter states:

A number of blacks and whites contend that equal educational opportunity does not require integration. While I have serious doubts about this thesis, . . . their views must be given serious consideration, and to hold such views should not be regarded as treason in civil rights circles. (27)

Although Carter feels that integrated education "must not be lost as the ultimate solution," he is concerned about the strategy of that quest which appears to destine "hundreds of thousands of black children . . . for the dunghill in our society" (27). For Carter, the current bottom line is clear:

> While we fashioned *Brown* on the theory that equal education and integrated education were one and the same, the goal was not integration but equal educational opportunity. Similarly, although the Supreme Court in 1954 believed that educational equality mandated integration, *Brown* requires equal educational opportunity. If that can be achieved without integration, *Brown* has been satisfied. (27)

3.) Cross states that his "nigrescence" (a French term which means "the process of becoming Black") model--"Negro-to-Black Conversion Model"--of the 1960s was, of course, influenced by the pathology inherent in the "self-hating Negro" concept so prevalent in social scientific literature. That concept suggested that there was the need for comprehensive personality and identity changes," although the "romanticism associated with Black nationalism" was an influencing factor in the desire for African Americans to assume a totally new identity. But, Cross' more recent insights into the fallacies of the "self-hatred" research and, especially, the input he received from students during discussions of nigrescence in one of his Princeton classes in the early 1970s, are contributing to his development of a new nigrescence model, which will include the previously overlooked theme of "continuity" (ix-x).

The strengths of African Americans that must continue in the conversion from Negro to Black became obvious as Cross' students pointed out that they could not identify as pathological the mental health of their "Negro" parents and relatives. In fact, Cross states, "some of the strengths the students identified in themselves, and that helped them account for their success at college, could be traced not to identity change but to their socialization by their (Negro) parents and extended families." And the students determined that "nigrescence" left them with some significant characteristics, while some key elements of their self-concept changed (xii). Cross states that the "distinction between personal identity ("general personality") and group identity ("reference group orientation") is crucial" to his analysis. He continues and states that:

> Research shows that until the onset of the so-called underclass, the material conditions of most working-class, middle-class, and even many poor Black families were such that parents were able to engender a great deal of psychological strength in their children and that this strength consistently manifested itself in psychological studies of Blacks as average scores on general personality measures. (xiv)

And in the Black Social Movement of the 1960s, he asserts, Black youth changed their ideologies but did not have to change already healthy personalities. He concludes:

> Such mental health was a legacy of the personal psychological victories that their parents were able to achieve and to pass on to the next generation via family socialization, the church, and the community. Building on this legacy of personal strength, young people in the 1960s unfolded a social movement that

54

pushed the community toward greater concensus on
what it means to be Black. (xiv)

Cross' emerging nigrescence model also embraces the
multitude of ideas and ideologies that Blacks have
always had about the significance of being Black.

The Racism Impediment

1.) Most of these analysts perceive the *Brown* phenomenon within the context of a racist society and
define that factor as a major impediment to effective
integration. Carter succinctly states:

> It was not until *Brown* I was decided that Blacks
> were able to understand that the fundamental vice
> was not legally enforced racial segregation itself;
> that this was a mere by-product, a symptom of the
> greater and more pernicious disease--white su-
> premacy. Needless to say, white supremacy is no
> mere regional contamination. It infects us nationwide
> and remains in the basic virus that has debilitated
> blacks' efforts to secure equality in this country. (23-24)

2.) Carter insists that the color question--even though
class is a factor--remains basic. More critically, he
expresses concern about the long-lasting effects of
contemporary racism, as Blacks are carefully selected
by the ruling class to assimilate into society's institutions in the post-Kennedy administration struggle to
appear a "multiracial society." This is a salient observation which is directly related to the writer's discourse and calls to mind the plight of Black journalist
Leanita McClain who, despondent, at least in part,
over a rude awakening to racism, committed suicide.

> Our institutions are no longer lily-white, and the
> process seems to be gaining momentum and increased

acceptance. But this does not preclude an even more insidious bias. Blacks who become executives, legislators, judges, corporate directors, managers, university professors are those who have the background and outlook similar to their white colleagues. Yet, even these establishment blacks are deeply affected by discrimination. Only future generations of social scientists and historians will be able to tell us whether the frustrations blacks encounter within the institutions of power they now serve will produce a more embittered social pathology than the one resulting from the policy of exclusion that was the norm in 1954. In short, class issues do have a negative impact on black and white relationships, but the race issue-- the color question-- remains basic. (25)

On the heels of review of these cogent analyses, the writer submits an observation about the following passage from the *Brown* decision, as cited in Richard Kluger's *Simple Justice* (1977):

Today, education is perhaps the most important function of state and local governments. . . It is the very foundation of good citizenship. Today it is a principal instrument in awakening the child to cultural values, in preparing him for later professional training, and in helping him to adjust normally to his environment. In these days, it is doubtful that any child may reasonably be expected to succeed in life if he is denied the opportunity of an education. Such an opportunity, where the state has undertaken to provide it, is a right which must be made available to all on equal terms. (781)

The role of education has generally been thus defined in twentieth-century American society. Culturally repressed, African Americans have internalized that philosophy of education and have thought that such education provided by Whites would surely equalize their social condition to that of White society. It is not surprising, then, that the NAACP Legal Defense Fund tactics relied on the testimony of social scientists to denounce segregated education as detrimental to the development of Black children.

On the surface, the entire passage quoted above appears to be unquestionably worthy of support by all Americans. If one is mindful of the mechanisms of internal colonialism, however, it will be clear that the purpose of education for a colonized people is first and foremost to perpetuate the condition of an inferior status. Thus, for White America to prepare African American children for ''good'' citizenship, to ''awaken'' them to cultural values, to prepare them for later ''professional training,'' and to help them adjust ''normally'' to their environment is a different matter than such preparation for White children; such preparation has always necessitated contrivance of duplicitous means in order to effect disparate ends.

Paradoxical Victory

Heralded by many, and severely criticized by some, the victory of *Brown* is a paradox. Although criticism of the NAACP litigation strategy which was ultimately fashioned is not ill-founded, the primary strategy--as Carter points out--focused on the inequities of the basic conditions of segregated education. An example of the strategy can be noted in *Briggs v. Elliott* (Clarendon County, South Carolina), one of the five cases argued before they were combined in the *Brown* litigation. In that litigation, Marshall asserted that the NAACP and the plaintiffs must be able to show that the state's segregation statutes as applied in the County were unconstitutional and to "show the inequalities as they actually exist." He pointed to the fact that although there were many more Black pupils attending public schools there than White pupils--three times as many, $395,000 a year was being spent on White pupils as compared to $282,000 being spent on Black students (Kluger, 348-49).

The introduction of the Clarks' doll-studies data had been viewed with skepticism by many within the NAACP legal team, but although this testimony was not well received in all of the cases, such testimony had proven helpful in the Kansas and Delaware cases (Kluger, 555). The NAACP team was faced with two main questions, according to Kluger:
(1) Should we attack *Plessy* head-on, simply telling the court that by every known standard of law and humanity it must be reversed, or should we try to dismiss it as irrelevant? (2) How much should we rely on the body of the social-science testimony gathered in the courts below? (553)

In the end, Marshall decided to use the doll-studies testimony data in the Supreme Court litigation, after Clark and his "two writing partners" prepared a paper that cited negative effects of segregation on the White community, including "a distorted sense of social reality," as well as "confusion, conflict, and moral cynicism" (556). The writing team garnered the signatures of 35 social scientists for the paper, including some from highly recognized American social scientists (557). Even though Marshall had been very concerned about using the Clarks' studies in earlier litigation in Briggs (South Carolina), he had decided that "on balance," the findings presented evidence that injury was done to Black children in segregated school settings (356). The unanswerable question remains: would the Court have ruled against segregated education had the doll-studies testimony not been introduced?

The NAACP strategy for and the Court's ruling on *Bolling v. Sharpe*, the District of Columbia school segregation case, bring that question sharply into focus. Strategy for this case compares interestingly to that for the other *Brown* cases. An entity free of any state authority, the District had established a segregated school system, although Congress had not made such a system mandatory. But, Congress had passed laws that seemed to foster continued school segregation and it was certainly aware of the practice in the District. Under Marshall's guidance, preparation for argument before the Court had involved Howard law school professors, with George E. C. Hayes and James Nabrit presenting before the Court. Their arguments focused on the racism inherent in segregation, segregation's deprivation of the liberty guaranteed all individuals under the Fifth Amendment's "due process" provision, and the fact that the Civil War Amendments declared that the federal government could have no power to make "racial distinctions" among its citizenry (Kluger, 577-78).

The Court issued a decision on *Bolling* separate from the *Brown* decision, declaring that the legal problem in the District of Columbia was different from that in the states. In *Brown*, the Court held that the Fourteenth Amendment granted equal protection to all individuals and thus prohibited the states from maintaining racially segregated schools. *Bolling* presented a different matter, the Court declared:

The Fifth Amendment, which is applicable in the District of Columbia, does not contain an equal protection clause as does the Fourteenth Amendment which applies only to the states. But the concepts of equal protection and due process, both stemming from our American ideal of fairness, are not mutually exclusive. The "equal protection of the laws" is a more explicit safeguard of prohibited unfairness than "due process of law," and, therefore, we do not imply that the two are always interchangeable phrases. But, as the Court has recognized, discrimination may be so unjustifiable as to be violative of due process. (Kluger, 786)

The Court logically concluded that no "lesser duty" could be imposed on the "Federal Government" than on the states, and held that "racial segregation in the public schools of the District of Columbia is a denial of the due process of law guaranteed by the Fifth Amendment to the Constitution" (Kluger, 787). Significantly, this determination was made without application of the *Brown* "psychological damage" theory.

Rather than the question of what decision the Court might have rendered had the NAACP *Bolling* strategy been applied in *Brown*, the overriding question now might be, for what better gain can that paradoxical victory be traded. Like segregation, integration was to be fashioned to maintain the status quo. However, under segregation, Black children were generally insulated from significant exposure to and confrontation with Whites. Cultural values and the virtues of Black citizenship were passed on generally by "seasoned" Black teachers and families--albeit colonized--most often committed to developing the "double consciousness" in their charges which could prepare them not only for psychological and physical survival, but for a generally meaningful existence within the context of a racist, segregated society. An aura of mystique surrounded the dominant society, since Blacks as a whole little understood the essence or function of most mores of that society. Under the integrated education which *Brown* projected, however, constant exposure to and contact with Whites, and inculcation of the White "world view" directly by Whites--and/or by Blacks thus "trained" by Whites--was to exacerbate an already dire situation, about which the Black community is now gravely concerned.

5

∶◆∶

THROUGH A GLASS DARKLY

WHITE LIBERALS, BLACK INTELLECTUALS

The social science data and testimony employed by the NAACP legal team in the *Brown* testimony, referred to in the preceding analyses of the *Brown* proceedings, warrant further review. It can be noted, first of all, that the very nature of the field of social science, within a colonial context, would seem to cast serious doubt as to the feasibility of the application of principles and research within those disciplines to support the quest for social justice by the colonized. Social science is, after all, composed of the various disciplines of study relating to the institutions and functioning of a society and the interaction of its individual members. In such a quest, the same can be said for the employment of the colonizer's legal system. The overriding Weltanschauung of White society reserves for itself the privilege of superiority and domination of non-Whites by Whites. Black social scientists, like other Black Americans (perhaps even more so, since they have formally studied the fields honed by Whites), have most often unwittingly internalized the code of

62

White superiority, seemingly unconscious of their own cultural repression. Furthermore, the alliance of Black and White social scientists who have sought to aid the cause of Black liberation has not been satisfactorily beneficial to Blacks. Social scientists James A. Tillman, Jr. and Mary Norman Tillman are among those in the field who are becoming increasingly aware of this dilemma. Two decades ago, these two scholars succinctly defined the role of White liberals and Black intellectuals in "racism's circle of conditioning-reinforcement-continuity-conditioning." They applied this analysis of racism in America in a 1972 *Phylon* article and also wrote:

> Black intellectuals and white liberals--however defined and of whatever variety--have played critical and crucial roles in shaping the race relations landscape of the United States. Because both groups have avowed their commitment to equal justice for blacks, their assumptions about goals, procedures and directions, with rare exceptions, have gone unexamined. This condition if permitted to continue can become counter-productive. ...On the whole, black intellectuals who have devoted their scholarly efforts and talents to the systematic study of American race relations, whether in the historic or contemporary context, have compounded and exacerbated the race relations picture in America. Thus, they have--wittingly or unwittingly--contributed to the virulence and spread of racial insanity in this country. (54)

A specific look at the alliance of White and Black social scientists for NAACP testimony in *Brown* and attention to the Black condition more than 30 years after *Brown* leaves one hard-pressed to reject this logic. *Simple Justice*, Kluger's exhaustive account of

63

the personalities and proceedings involved in a ''cluster of cases''--a total of five--prosecuted by the NAACP that eventually came to be referred to as *Brown v. Board of Education,* indicates that NAACP lawyers employed more than 100 witnesses for testimony throughout *Brown* (420, 777). Within the team of social scientists who prepared and/or presented testimony, there were two whose testimony indubitably rocked the boat: Black social psychologist Kenneth B. Clark (353) and White assistant professor of psychology at Kansas University Louisa Pinkham Holt, who had also been associated with the highly-regarded Topeka Menninger institute of psychiatry (419-420).

No testimony, Kluger writes, ''had a more detectable impact on the phrasing of the final court decision in *Brown*'' than that of Holt with regard to the effect of legally-sanctioned segregation on Black children (420-21). Holt purported that such segregation engendered a ''sense of inferiority'' in Black children which adversely affected ''motivation for learning.'' Moreover, she proffered, the earlier in life such a significant event occurred, the ''more lasting, the more far-reaching and deeper the effects'' (421-22). Clearly, some passages in the Court's decision which have been quoted here reflect these phrases. These concepts reinforced the testimony of other social scientists. The testimonies of Holt and of Clark reinforced each other and, like Holt's testimony, Clark's testimony, based on the doll-studies data produced by him and his wife, had critical implications for the outcome of *Brown.*

Kenneth B. Clark had prepared a paper for the 1950 White House Mid-century Conference on Youth, solicited by his former Howard University professor Alain Locke, which was based upon the Clarks' doll and coloring tests. Kluger states that Clark's White House paper pointed out that other social scientists had conducted similar research. Kluger notes non-Black Marian J. Radke and Helen G. Trager, whose tests he describes as more elaborate than the Clarks'. Five years after the White House conference, the report was published in revised form as a book, *Prejudice and Your Child* (318). The Supreme Court opinion cited Clark's White House report - *Effect of Prejudice and Discrimination on Personality Development*-- listing it first in ''Footnote #11'' among seven works by social scientists mentioned in the NAACP legal briefs during litigation of the school cases (705-6). ''Footnote #11'' was to become, Kluger states, ''one of the most debated in the annals of the Court'' (705). As noted earlier, the conclusions which the Clarks' studies formed were, and remain, highly controversial. Moreover, the similarity of the correlation of data to conclusions in the earlier works of some White social scientists and liberals, as well as in that of other *Brown* social science testimony, credence to the allegation of the perpetuation of the ''circle of racism'' which Tillman and Tillman posit.

Kluger reports that although Clark's research data were unchallenged at the time of testimony, they were not to remain unchallenged before the ''cluster of cases'' were spent, both in court proceedings and by a number of other commentators (355). And as noted earlier, the NAACP lawyers and Clark himself had been concerned about the interpretation well before the testimony was presented (356).

It is understandable that since the stakes were so high, NAACP lawyers and the social science team felt that the doll-studies evidence, though questionable, did seem to reinforce an already accepted tenet and was well worth whatever risks it might harbor. At rock bottom, however, the phenomenon of the acceptance of the doll-studies findings represents a major symptom of what ails futile attempts to significantly improve the lot of Black Americans: the dogma of White superiority/Black inferiority that blinds reason, incites individuals as well as the society to immorality and even criminal acts, and propels all social sense and action to the honor and glory of that end. The writer submits that African Americans involved in *Brown*, the African American social science witnesses and attorneys, were in the grips of psychological occupation, like other African Americans. Moreover, because of their professional training, the psyches of these witnesses and of the African American legal professionals might have been more misoriented than psyches of the average African American. Are we to assume that these professionals and the court personnel both believed, however disparate the reasons, that Blacks are inferior to Whites, that the separation of the races--whether mandatory or voluntary--is injurious to Blacks because it prevents Blacks from gaining necessary attributes that could only be acquired by association with Whites-- one of the most significant of which is a psychological feeling of worth? Deference to the White world view was reflected in the reasoning employed by African Americans in critical *Brown* proceedings. Educated away from the essential quest for the preservation of the group, as through a glass darkly, African Americans have historically forged and/or supported strategies and policies which have negatively impacted upon African American welfare. Another significant factor in the accommodationist attitude of Blacks has been a lack of understanding of the distinction between the rhetoric of democratic ideals and the duplicity of the Constitution, law, and the practice of democracy in America. Kluger reports the reaction of Alfred H. Kelly, who was chairman of the history department at Wayne State University in Detroit when he assisted in research for the NAACP *Brown* team (626), to the qualities of intellectual adequacy and political naivete he noted in the team's Black civil rights advocates:

> During the intensive sessions, Kelly was struck by two not quite contradictory qualities in the black men who sat around the table with him. ''If I had ever entertained any lurking white-man's suspicion of the intellectual adequacy of this group of lawyers, all but one or two of whom were Negroes, these men soon kicked it out of me,'' Kelly later said. ''Without exception, they were razor-keen, deadly at argumentation, and, as far as a layman who knew some law could tell, thoroughly competent in their profession.'' But there was that other quality that frankly surprised Kelly: ''In a sense, these men were profoundly naive. They really felt that once the legal barriers fell, the whole black-white situation would change. I was more skeptical, but they were convinced that the relationship between the law and society was the key. There was a very conservative element in these men then in the sense that they really believed in the American dream and that it could be made to work for black men, too.'' (639)

About Thurgood Marshall, Kelly states:

> Thurgood Marshall was--and is--an American patriot. He truly believed in the United States and the Constitution, but that the whole system was tragically flawed by the segregation laws. Wipe away those laws and the whole picture would change. Marshall and his

colleagues were no rebels. They felt that the social order was fundamentally good. What they wanted was the chance to share in it like men." (639)

But, Marshall indicated, prior to his retirement as a Supreme Court Justice, his understanding of the problems of racism and injustice in America. For example, in a televised interview with African American journalist Carl Rowan (1987), he declared that African Americans are "not free yet." (1987)

Kluger himself writes of a social reality which is seldom introduced in the classroom: "the proclaimed equality of all men and their inalienable right to life, liberty, and the pursuit of happiness had made the Declaration of Independence one of history's undying humanitarian statements. But no such exalted declarations had found their way into the much more business like Constitution." He notes the "tactful, tacit racism of the Constitution," somewhat modified "beginning with adoption of the Thirteenth Amendment in 1865 and culminating in passage of the Civil Rights Act of 1875" (626).

Scientific Colonialism

It is clear that Black social scientists have had specific education in the principles of fields in which data can too easily be manipulated, and sometimes fraudulently and purposefully, by proponents of colonization. Thus, as indicated earlier by the writer, they and others of the older generations have not escaped psychological manipulation by the dominant society and the younger generations are paying doubly for this fact.

Knowledge of one particular scientific fraud is significantly alarming, from the writer's perspective, to shatter at least the outer layer of psychological occupation of African Americans: the work and legacy of twentieth-century English psychologist Sir Cyril Burt. There is no more classic example of the kind of scientific colonialism that has impacted upon the Black psyche and life, as well as upon that of other oppressed people, than that exercised by Burt. Sir Cyril Burt held the "most prestigious" chair of psychology at University College, London, from 1932 until his death, at 88, in 1971 (Guthrie 1980, 17). Respected as dean of the hereditarians, a scholar whose theories of intelligence had influenced the total education system in Great Britain as well as that of other countries--Burt was uncovered as a fraud shortly after his death.

In 1979, *Psychology Today* published a review by Harvard scientist Steven Jay Gould of a major work by English psychologist L. S. Hearnshaw on the life of Cyril Burt, *Cyril Burt, Psychologist* (Gould 104-105). The review noted one of Burt's findings, the "most persuasive data supporting the innatest claim: remarkably high correlations of IQ between siblings for 53 pairs of identical twins separated at or near birth and raised apart in different environments--the only reasonably natural experiment available for testing the hereditarian hypothesis in human beings. No other investigation had managed to amass even half as many cases of this rara avis." The review detailed how Burt's "edifice began to crumble" shortly after his death, as Princeton psychologist Leon Kamin began scrutinizing Burt's work.

Leon Kamin noticed that although Burt increased his sample of identical twins from 15 to 53 in several sequential papers, his correlation co-efficients remained unchanged to the third decimal place--a virtual impossibility if Burt had really added new data to his sample. Then, Oliver Gillie presented more damaging evidence, which could not be attributed to mere carelessness. Among other things, Burt's two most important coauthors and supposed compilers of the data on twins either did not exist at all or could not have been in contact with Burt while he did the work. (104)

Pointing out that there were further irregularities, and that some supporters, including psychologist Arthur Jensen, had attempted to come to Burt's defense, the article stated: "One must . . . ask why so many people are willing to clutch at the skimpiest of straws to support the tired and discredited argument of strict hereditarianism" (104).

One of the most critical applications of Burt's work--and certainly one of the most socially detrimental--has been by long-time professor at the University of California-Berkeley, Arthur R. Jensen. Jensen's "research-based" theory of "genetic determinism" clings to the notion of the innate inferior intelligence of Blacks vis-a-vis Whites, which is, he asserts, clearly evidenced in IQ testing and other such measurements of intelligence (1969, See references in Miller 1980, 66-67; White 1980, 5; Weinberg, 1983, 70-74).

A 1976 *Newsweek* article noted above reported that disciple Jensen had taken a more charitable view of Burt's failings than had Kamin, that he had "attributed them to Burt's age, his crankiness, and his admittedly failing memory." The article quoted Jensen: "It is almost as if Burt regarded the actual data as merely incidental backdrop for the illustration of the theoretical issues." Perhaps the same could be said for the

Clarks' doll studies. A coauthor of the article revealed that two researchers who had worked with Burt in the 1940s and 50s had been, "suspicious about Burt's integrity even then." (Panati with Mac Pherson, 1976).

Burt represents but one example of a centuries-old phenomenon, and one about which Blacks world-wide have been generally too unconcerned. However, the consequences of such colonialism are beginning to come into sharper focus. The contradictions of the colonized mind is a consequence of major concern. Cross' review, in *Shades of Black*, of the development of the theory of Black self-hate reveals the influence of scientific colonialism. He indicates the "predisposition" of White researchers to identify low self-esteem, self-hatred, and anti-Blackness in the average African American, which Kenneth Clark and his associates announced in the early 1950s (115). Cross points to the distorted research and theorizing which flowed from a string of social scientists. Ruth Horowitz, it appears, was influenced by Kurt Lewin, who had earlier referred to the American Negroes as exhibiting the "better known and most extreme cases of self-hatred," and offered as a solution to "this dilemma" the need to belong "to a group whose fate has a positive meaning" (13).

Early in the twentieth century, John E. Lind and A.B. Evarts, psychiatrists in Washington, D.C., at what is now St. Elizabeth's Hospital, wrote about the "color complex" with which "Negroes" were afflicted, even in the absence of psychosis. And Lind seemed inclined toward the work of the German Alfred Adler, who was examining the assumption of European Jewish self-hatred, advanced a thesis on the "sense of inferiority and the will to power" (5). Lewin transported the Jewish "self-hatred" theme to America and

71

his work found a place in *The Mark of Oppression* (Kardiner and Ovesey, 1951) which, as noted earlier, sealed the self-hating Negro theme in social scientific literature and ultimately influenced the Clarks' research findings. Cross makes a point about the self-esteem of some of those non-Blacks who branded Blacks as self-hating: he notes that the Horowitzes changed their name to "Hartley," apparently about 1947; another figure in the discourse on the meaning of Negro identity--Eric Homburg--changed his name to "Erick H. Erickson;" "and Alfred Adler"--"from whom such terms as "self-image" and "inferiority complex" came, "had himself baptized" as a young man, although he was born a Jew (15-16).

Cross reports that the theme continues to affect the research of African Americans, as is evident in the work of a young scholar--D. Powell-Hopson--who replicated the Clarks' Doll Test, using the popular Cabbage Patch Doll. The test, she reported, indicated the continued self-hatred tendency of Black children. Cross notes that the particular doll is one of the "most commercially successful in the history of toy manufacturing", and that, though it comes in both a Black and a White version, the doll given most prominence in the manufacturer's advertising campaigns was the White doll; thus it constituted one of the least stimulus-neutral dolls ever employed in a racial-preference study. As many Black parents have discovered, Black children, on being given the Black doll, very often come to like "it," but they often long for the "real" doll. (115-16)

Cross cites the wide reporting of the study in the media, and particularly of the fact that Powell-Hopson indicated that she "intervened" and brought the children to a "better mental state and outlook" by the end of the study by developing a Black preference in the Black children. But, in the end, the White children also exhibited preference for the Black doll! Scientific colonialism serves a clear purpose in a colonialist, racist society: it undergirds the perpetuation of the myth of the inferiority of the colonized and of the superiority of the colonizer.

Dialectics of the Colonized Mind

Among Black professionals, there has been for some time are cognized bit of wit, stated in jest, but internalized as a bitter fact: If you are Black in America and not schizophrenic, you must be crazy. It is difficult for American Blacks to maintain touch with reality, given the Black social condition; and those Blacks who are not aware of that reality are not making adequate use of their "left mind" (Hord 1974, 15-16). Some of the writer's perceptions of the contradictions of the colonized mind follow. Such perceptions are drawn here from the image of two prominent African American figures: Psychologist Kenneth B. Clark, and a more recent public figure, the late Clarence M. Pendleton, who was at the time of his sudden death in 1988 chairperson of the United States Commission on Civil Rights.

Kenneth Clark articulated his "integration" posture in a 1982 interview with *The New Yorker* magazine. He remains, he stated, "an incorrigible" or "rigid, hard-line integrationist." He clings to the concept of idealistic integration, seemingly convinced that the more integrated the situation--that is, the more the African American child is in the minority in his/her environment--the better he/she will be taught and able to learn. Some Black friends, Clark stated, urge him to

73

be more "pragmatic", but have not been able to dissuade him from this stance. In this same interview, however, Clark decried the worsening condition of the education of urban Blacks since *Brown*. He contrasted the turbulence of the 60s with what is happening today. Black children of the 80s are, "being destroyed silently, in the first and second grades" (73). Clark bemoans, it would seem, a phenomenon that was set in motion as the first generation or two of Black students were directly affected by *Brown* and its extensions.

But there appears to be for Clark, as with most African Americans of his generation, that certain "double-consciousness" and experiential understanding that often induces apparent contradictions in behavior, reflecting the dialectics of the colonized mind. Adhering to the ideal of integration, Clark boasted of the fact that he resigned from the board of directors of Antioch College "because the College had supported the creation on its campus of a racially exclusive Afro-American Institute" (64). Yet, Clark exhibited another consciousness as he described the perspective and method used in one of the undertakings of the consulting firm he formed--Clark, Phipps, Clark, and Harris, Inc.--which "quickly attracted clients from both government and business who needed help in designing affirmative action programs and in solving other problems in race relations" (67). The *New Yorker* article explains:

> Projects have been completed for American Telephone & Telegraph (one was a study of minority students in college who are majoring in the disciplines from which the corporation does its hiring) and an international engineering consulting firm. "On the basis of our selection process," Clark said,

"they are hiring as draftsmen and designers young-
sters who would not ordinarily be employed by them
but who have potential. We turn the young people
over to the consulting firm for training, but during
that period we provide them with support and coun-
seling--on any kind of problem, personal or profes-
sional--and also monitor the training program. Included are blacks, Hispanics, Asians, and some
whites. As you can see, this is not what you'd call an
ordinary business" (68).

And so, Clark and Associates shelter, fend for and
apparently give training in self-help and in surviving
the effects of discrimination and lack of understanding
to these vulnerable young, for common sense and long
years in the experience of struggle against racial as well
as economic oppression dictate that such an approach
will likely promote more success in the long run than
blind assimilation, or a hands-off, monitor-and-advise-
only approach.

In *The New Yorker* interview referred to above,
Clark spoke of the vigorous standards he was subjected to as an undergraduate student of psychology at
Howard University and of how Professor Cecil Francis
Sumner would tolerate ''no nonsense about there being anything like 'Black psychology'--any more than
he would have allowed any nonsense about 'black
astronomy'' (45). Unfortunately until more recent years,
this kind of thinking among the vast majority of Black
intellectuals was all too prevalent, as noted earlier
above, since ''universal'' knowledge had been passed
on to Blacks by self-appointed ''universal man.'' As-
tutely, in *Dark Ghetto*, published 11 years after *Brown*,
Clark defines urban Black ghettos as ''social, political,
educational, and above all--economic colonies'' (1965, 11).

However, his seemingly preferred solution of having African American children and educators more in the minority in integrated education is at odds with the internal colonialism model, which places much of the blame for cultural repression and thus, oppression of a people, on the colonizer's control of the institutions of socialization. Clark's stance and ideals have been entirely sincere, however, and indicative of one who is self-respecting and who deserves respect. Moreover, his influence has been a very positive factor for Blacks in a number of situations--including *Brown*. Were the agonies of much of the integration effort less prevalent, one might be tempted to sympathize with Clark's idealistic tenacity.

Cross makes some interesting observations about the perspective of Mamie and Kenneth Clark. A significant point is that they have not been ''experts'' on ''Negro culture,'' and do not understand its complexities, but have been called upon to give analyses of that culture. They have seen ''Negroness'' as a stigma, he observes, and this has affected their research and analyses, and caused them to be very ''unhappy'' about the Black identity movement in the 1960s and 1970s, for they viewed it as ''a sign of reactionary separatism.'' They saw no merit, he contends, in Black culture and produced an image of the ''Negro dominated by feelings of inferiority.'' What they did provide, he notes, is ''extraordinary insight into what happens when racism cripples the mind and spirit,'' but Kenneth Clark, particularly, in his writings, gave no indication that ''Negro culture'' had any positive and effective mechanisms for transcending racism'' (36-37).

The employment of the colonized who have either wittingly or unwittingly become crusading disciples for the colonizers has become an alarmingly effective tactic. This was especially true under the two-term 1980s administration of President Ronald Reagan. One such significant example cannot be omitted here. The late Clarence Pendleton--the Reagan administration's chairperson of the United States Commission Civil Rights--exhibited the contradictions of the colonized mind, like Kenneth Clark, but appeared to lack the sincerity, intelligence, and self-respect of Clark.

Pendleton asserted that Black leaders who seek race-conscious remedies for their social problems and who demand government support for economic remedies are "peddling pain and not progress, because Americans spoke in the last election (the election of Ronald Reagan)--conservative Americans." At the same time, he spoke of some problems of Blacks stemming from their not having protected their own institutions after *Brown* (Reynolds, March 6, 1985, 11A) which is indicative of his comprehension of the need for race-conscious approaches on the part of Blacks as they seek to solve their social problems. This would imply that such approaches are also appropriate for government. However, Pendleton supported the Reagan administration posture that Blacks do not need "special treatment" through Affirmative Action and other such considerations, that they can and do achieve positions of significant employment as a whole through sheer merit. Such assertions on the part of a number of Blacks-- those who sincerely believe this and are not just parroting this for personal gain--are vivid manifestations of the kind of psychological occupation and/or ignorance of past and present reality that is not significantly apparent in other oppressed, though not as significantly culturally repressed, American groups.

77

Have White females, for example, promulgated any such significant denial of their need for or right to redress for past wrongs, and the need for justice in the present, through the exercise of Affirmative Action? Examples of such denial are hard to find. Most significantly, White females have benefited the most from Affirmative Action initiatives.

Pendleton and his President appeared to have joined hands in the use of a criticism leveled by Booker T. Washington at Frederick Douglass, in order to keep Blacks confused and divided. Of course, such tactics, designed to keep working-class Whites fighting among themselves, have long been affected by the ruling classes in order to cloud enlightenment as to the role of the elite in the misery of the masses. In 1985, Reagan declared a group of little-known Black "conservatives" to be "leaders" as he invited them to the White House to discuss solutions to Black America's problems (Marable 1985, 26). These "leaders" helped to reinforce Pendleton's spiel, using the kind of criticism which Bernard R. Boxill's article "Self-Respect and Protest" in *Philosophy Born of Struggle* (1983) cites as having been used by early 19th century educator Booker T. Washington with regard to Douglass:

> Washington, for example, criticized Frederick Douglass for constantly reminding black people of "their sufferings" and suspected that persistent protesters relied on "the special sympathy of the world" rather than on "their own efforts." This is an important charge since the self-respecting person is self-reliant and avoids self-pity. (191-192)

Boxill continues with an interpretation which projects the fallacies in Washington's stance (as well as in Pendleton and his cohorts):

It is not answered by the claim that people have rights, for having rights does not necessarily justify constant reiteration that one has them. The charge is answered, however, by a closer consideration of what is involved in claiming a right. The idea that the protester seeks sympathy is unlikely since in claiming his rights he affirms that he is claiming what he can demand and exact, and sympathy cannot be demanded and exacted. The idea that the protester is self-pitying is likewise implausible, since a person who feels pity for himself typically believes that his condition is deplorable and unavoidable, and this is not at all what the protester affirms. On the contrary, he affirms that his condition is avoidable, he insists that what he protests is precisely the illegitimate, and hence avoidable, interference by others in the exercise of his rights, and he expresses the sentiment, not of self-pity, but of resentment. (192)

Political sociologist Manning Marable in a February, 1985 Editorial Commentary in the *The National Leader* suggested that Pendleton might well have received the nod of approval from Reagan in the President's search for a "new" Booker T., given some of Pendleton's speeches. Marable noted that:

Pendleton's recent speeches have made the original Uncle Tom look like Malcolm X. He claims that Afro-Americans have made "tremendous progress" under Reagan and has even compared Jesse Jackson, NAACP leader Benjamin Hooks and other national Black leaders to the murderous evangelist Jim Jones. Reagan's budget cuts and tax policies are "designed to take Blacks on the pathway to glory, from rags to riches, from poverty to parity." But Pendleton's hyperbolic posturing and sorry inability to comprehend the deterioration of Blacks' socio-economic conditions during the past four years negate his potential to lead anyone anywhere. (26)

Marable concluded that Pendleton could not fill Washington's shoes:

> The President's frustrated efforts to create a docile Black "leadership" in the image of Booker T. Washington are futile for two basic reasons. Historically, Booker T. Washington was no Uncle Tom, despite his accommodationist rhetoric. Secretly, he lobbied against segregation codes, and he financed Black economic and political institutions which strengthened the Black community. Washington championed industrial education for Blacks, but sent his own daughter to elite private schools. He accepted Jim Crow railroad cars, but always traveled in the first class sections. Despite legal disenfranchisement, Washington and the Tuskegee Institute faculty continued to vote in Alabama during the early 1900s. The tragedy of Booker T. Washington was that his accommodationist strategy in the long run could not overturn racial discrimination and economic oppression. The tragedy for these new Black conservatives is that they lack even the subtle duplicity of Washington. (26)

It seems that there are, on every front, Blacks-- whether male or female, or of Pendleton's generation or younger--guilty of Pendletonian atrocities of deception and/or ignorance. The young Uncle Toms of the 80s did not necessarily "shuffle along" they were more likely to swing along an elite avenue--or throughout the campuses of academia--to a "Buppie" song. Contemporary Uncle Tomism is congruent with contemporary racism. Even more controversial and ominous than Clarence Pendleton is Associate Supreme Court Justice Clarence Thomas, whose nomination was confirmed by the Senate in 1991, after a tumultuous, unprecedented Senate hearing. Although President George Bush declared that Thomas was the "best qualified" person in the land, many African Americans and White Americans accused Bush of an appointment based solely on the "color of the skin" rather than on qualifications. The President's action was incredible to many, given his grandstand opposition to Affirmative Action "quotas" (even where none were evidenced as in the 1990 Civil Rights Act, which he vetoed, claiming that it was a "quota bill"). The Thomas appointment had every appearance of being the typical bad faith Affirmative Action selection.

Given Thomas' relative lack of significant experience as a jurist, as well as his adamant stance against some basic tenets for relief of poverty and oppression, most ironic is the fact that Thomas was appointed to replace a distinguished African American Associate Supreme Court Justice, the late Thurgood Marshall, who had become a legend in his own time. Bush surely anticipated that this nomination would cause some concern on the part of civil rights advocates. But, what resulted was a national furor pregnant with a number of explosive issues--in the African American community and in the national political climate.

President Bush proved to be even more crafty than President Reagan, whom he succeeded, wreaking considerable havoc in the civil rights arena during his one term. There seems little doubt that Bush's appointment of Clarence Thomas was calculated to pacify the African American populace while continuing the Reagan-Bush strategy of catering to the dominant society's growing anti-minority attitude. Bush seemed to depend on the African American camaraderie of color for support of Thomas, in spite of Thomas' anti-Affirmative Action record as Assistant Secretary for Civil Rights in the U.S. Department of Education (1981-82) and as Chairman of Equal Employment Opportunity Commission (1982-90). In the end, that spirit of camaraderie seemed to prevail, although prominent groups such as the NAACP and the Congressional Black Caucus strongly opposed the appointment.

But, it was apparent that much of the final support resulted due to what many African Americans perceived as an attack on Thomas in the incredible development of a sexual harassment claim by African American law professor Anita Hill, who had worked under Thomas in both the Department of Education and the EEOC. Much of the attention by African Americans, as well as by others, to the televised Senate confirmation hearings developed at the point of the introduction of Anita Hill's dramatic allegation. Even though Thomas had very often decried even apparently valid claims of racial discrimination by African Americans, faced with questioning by the Senate Committee about Ms. Hill's charge of sexual harassment, Thomas conveniently resorted to that very charge; he went so far as to compare his treatment to a "high-tech lynching" of a Black man.

Many came to feel protective of the "brother" subjected to the explicitly embarrassing accusations voiced by Ms. Hill before a White, male Senate Committee ill-prepared to conduct the sensitive investigation at hand. Such basis for galvanization is understandable, but costly in the context of contemporary racism and neocolonialism. For many knew little or nothing about Thomas' professional record or competency, or of his declaration of contempt for the likes of poor African Americans who would not pull themselves up by their own bootstraps, as he claimed to have done. And some dismissed such knowledge as secondary to allegiance to skin color, with little thought to what effect such attitudes might have on judicial decisions, if the Thomas appointment was to be confirmed.

Prior to the introduction of the sexual harassment claim, during confirmation proceedings Thomas' strategy for building his image focused on relating the fact of his humble but honorable upbringing and his success in pulling himself up by his own bootstraps. Reared by poor grandparents in Pin Point, Georgia, Thomas credited his grandfather, who he has stated was strict to the point of beating him, with developing in him the courage to stand up for himself and the ability to overcome the obstacles of segregation through hard work and self-reliance, without the crutches of dependency on special help. Thomas' bootstrap claim gave grist to those who would blame all poor African Americans for their own plight, no matter what the circumstances. However, so many prominent African Americans had humble beginnings, that even though Thomas' White mentors and the Senate Confirmation Hearing Committee were impressed, the "humble background" references began to wear thin and public ridicule of the "bootstrap" image forced Thomas to finally abandon this claim. He had received financial aid to attend Yale law school, as well as what appeared special consideration, in the fact of limited judicial experience, in the Supreme Court appointment.

Clarence Thomas seems to have been brutally affected by the racism he has encountered and exhibits what one journalist, Courtland Milloy, has referred to as self-contempt (1991, D3), in noting that Thomas had once even publicly ridiculed his own sister's dependence at one point on public aid. But Thomas displays a duality which permits him to commit such acts, to cater to the special interests of Whites on whom he depends for sponsoring and fostering his career advancement, and to reject Blackness and any laws and initiatives intended to negate the past and present effects of racial discrimination--even those which have benefited him personally.

The NAACP's opposition statement to Thomas' appointment noted "the two sides" of Judge Thomas. The organization referred to his earlier writings, which they pointed out sent "mixed signals" on his civil rights views, and to his two distinctly different views on "several important constitutional issues." Furthermore, the organization made clear that its stand was based on principle, not color, pointing out that it had opposed Judge Bork's nomination (he was not confirmed) and Associate Justices Scalia and Souter, who presented similar profiles. It would appear "both inconsistent and race-based" to support Thomas, the NAACP declared, "because we would be giving Thomas the benefit of our doubts, even though his opposition to positions of importance to us is, in many ways, more strident and articulate than that of previous nominees" (NAACP, 1991, 3, 4).

It is not easily determined whether Thomas is fully conscious of this duality, whether or not he uses it for his own advancement, or is only a victim of the psychological impact of racism and what Milloy terms "survival rearing," and his reported feeling of being rejected by many African Americans as well as Whites

(D3). Milloy's reference to a statement Thomas made to the conservative Heritage Foundation in 1987 would indicate that Thomas is conscious of the racism he has endured, and that he has consciously determined how he will play the game, even though that game plan may be bitter medicine. Thomas is quoted:

> Often it seemed that to be accepted within the conservative ranks and to be treated with some degree of acceptance, a black was required to become a caricature of sorts, providing sideshows of anti-black quips and attacks. (D3)

What better indication of an impaired psyche than one who, recognizing this degrading phenomenon, continues to perform, apparently not in the interest of some noble cause, but in the interest of "acceptance" by the very source of degradation and oppression? But, given the history of his life that Thomas presented, it appears that he has been shaped by mentors of the dominant society (for example, White catholic nuns in elementary school, professors in college and law school, politicians) for such a role, throughout his integrated education and career.

Clarence Thomas' particular previously expressed views on contemporary controversial issues (which he guarded well during the confirmation hearing), including Affirmative Action, the right to privacy, and abortion, drew opposition to his appointment from many sources, including religious, civil rights, labor, and women's groups. But, his appointment was ultimately confirmed by a befuddled Senate, in a close vote. The sexual harassment charge may have been opportune, for it will not be known whether or not the Thomas appointment would have been confirmed if that charge had not altered the course of events. But, Bush had arranged a situation, as is so often done, in which "the Blacks" could "fight it out" and he and his constituents would not lose, whatever the outcome.

Given the neocolonialist strategy of appointing or electing authority figures from among the colonized who will assist the colonizer in controlling the colonized and promoting the colonizer's interests, Thomas' appointment should not have been surprising to African Americans. Of the many scholarly and journalistic analyses the Thomas appointment has so far generated, among those pertinent to the themes of internal colonialism/neocolonialism are observations by civil rights advocate attorney Derrick Bell and novelist and poet Sarah E. Wright. Bell speaks to Thomas' advocacy for the Bush administration's "blame-the-victim" opposition to government help for the poor working class, while enthusiastically supporting "policies that further the already enormous gap between the rich and the rest of American citizenry."

Most significantly, Bell points to a sickness portrayed in Thomas' actions that the writer interprets as something akin to the psychological occupation malady addressed in this discourse. Bell submits:

The espousal of such views by an intelligent black man with access to all the facts, reflects a racial oppression-related malady far more serious than the welfare dependency against which Judge Thomas inveighs with such passion. (1991, 2)

Wright points out that in the confirmation hearings, the "Establishment, the politicians, and the media" framed the "issues according to their liking," focusing on the sexual harassment claim and diverting the public from the "real deal." Wright points to the disturbing real deal, which the writer submits is the neocolonialist tactic.

> For behind the Thomas nomination is the conspiracy of the right wing to create a layer of black collaborationists, to ensure their placement in positions of influence and to guarantee that they are conspicuously rewarded for their collaboration and are then to constitute the new "role models" for aspiring black people. The Thomas nomination, and now confirmation, sends out the message to African Americans that if they are willing to preach the virtues of rugged individualism and to oppose aspirations of the masses of black people, their careers will be well greased. (1992, 226)

This conspiracy exists not only at such high governmental levels, but in the workplace and other institutions of our society. African Americans must be attuned to this phenomenon and willing to combat it, realizing that to support "brothers" and "sisters" primarily on the basis of skin color, when they are obviously being used as puppets for various degrees of oppression, is an unaffordable folly.

Many older-generation Blacks who have not been guilty of Pendletonian or Uncle Thomas atrocities are not without blame, however, for the worsening condition of Black youth. Many who often blame the young for losing their identity and ideals; who brand some as shiftless; who bemoan the irony of some of these descendants of slaves adopting the same set of values that were responsible for the enslavement of their ancestors are, in their inertness, just as much accomplices in the tragedy as the framers and implementors of *Brown*. For they have, more often than not, proudly rendered to the dominant society the responsibility for nurturing their young. Even more tragic than the older generations' abdication of such responsibility is the prospect that each future generation of the young will lack even the wherewithal to nurture their children.

Education and "Manifest Destiny"

Clearly, the general educational, economic, political, and physical detriment of Black America is not what was envisioned by those African Americans who in the 1950s and 1960s struggled to promote civil rights legislation and judicial decisions which would promote equality for Black America. Since the abolishment of legalized slavery, constitutional amendments, executive orders (such as President Lyndon Johnson's 1965 Executive Order 11246 which implemented Affirmative Action), and judicial decisions have ostensibly provided remedies--albeit incremental--for the social maladies which White America has for centuries inflicted upon Black America. But, the logic of these measures has generally circumvented confrontation with one of the most serious maladies rooted in this society: the assumption of White superiority and White rule.

This malady seems to have resulted in and be perpetuated by two disabling social addictions with which White America and Black America are afflicted, each of which complements the other: Whites are addicted to the "manifest destiny" (see White, Parham, and Parham 1980, 63; Kennedy 1989, 246-360) of White supremacy--cultural, political, economic, and physical domination of people of color throughout the world. Blacks have seemed addicted to tolerating this domination, in one form or another, adjusting their very souls to accommodate colonization and dependency. In the United States of America, each of these phenomena has been exacerbated by *Brown* and by *Adams*.

Ideally, Black and White Americans might squarely face the egregious problem of White domination and Black accommodation and forge a system of education which prescribes an appropriate alexipharmac for these deadly opiates. The denial syndrome must first be shed and realistic analyses effected. However, the quest for a solution to this American dilemma is not likely to pursue such a path. Moreover, indications are that too many educators of the dominant society are continuing means to covertly--and sometimes blatantly overtly-- instruct their progeny in the wiles and ways of domination/oppression.

The most important educational factor is not the facilities or race of your

6

BECOMING OF
ONE MIND

Although Blacks have endured cultural repression and psychological assault since their enslavement in America, the anticipated promise of the *Brown* mandate--the contrived integration of the Black and White races in schooling on a national basis--has rudely evolved into the further subjugation of Black people the civil right won--the colonizer's logic, language, and chosen means of the implementation of the *Brown* decision actually reflecting the psychological occupation of African Americans--engendered the further erosion of the right of Black America to the psychological autonomy which preserves group history and heritage and promotes groups survival and fulfillment.

Thus confronted with this massive problem, Black America must wage yet a new struggle, one that will regroup its energies in order to recoup the Black psyche from various conditions of detriment. Valiant one-by-one and one-on-one efforts to counteract the erosion of the African American spirit and personality notwithstanding, the writer calls upon Black America to develop and support collective leadership which can assert a collective ethos/perspective purpose, and plan, that can revitalize the African American "survival thrust" (Baldwin 1985, 216-222 passim). The initial focus of this leadership should serve to define and foster, for captive African American youth in schools and colleges, comprehensive institutionalization of a philosophical nexus between African American traditions and values and African Americans in integrated institutions of education--at all levels. And most critically, for such an undertaking, this leadership will of necessity be not bound by the Euro-American ethos, perception of reality, and modes of functioning. Herein lies the crux of the matter--the alpha and the omega: essentially, becoming of one mind. This latter consideration is, of course, central to implementing and sustaining efforts to achieve a collective effort to halt the disintegration of a "functional" (Russell Adams, telephone interview, September 20, 1987) African American "presence." The African American--or Black--presence must exemplify more than the mere physical proximity of Americans of African descent. An African American mind imbued with African American values and purpose is key to a functional African American presence. For African Americans, there must be abundant experiences which revitalize and sustain cultural memory; experiences which reinforce the African American psyche with prescience critical to collective behavior which will effect an empowered presence. An empowered Black/African American presence contributes to the preservation of the African American individual and to the African American community as a cohesive and viable entity. This is a tall order, given the bizarre evolution of the status of people of African descent in the twentieth century, globally as well as nationally.

Self-help Efforts

Although there were various attempts during the early years following *Brown* and *Adams* to address perceived problems of Black students in integrated/desegregated educational settings, few viable solutions were forthcoming. The perception of problems, as well as solutions, was too often informed by the "psychologistic," or socio-psychological (Howie, 373), premise of the *Brown* decision and, therefore, inherently faulty. At the same time, too many of the sound efforts proposed or initiated were demeaned and/or dismantled, through either lack of understanding or malevolence, by Blacks as well as by Whites. Moreover, successful African American "self-help" endeavors in education, as well as in other institutions, have often proven embarrassing to the dominant group, vis-`a-vis their apparent inability to have effected similar outcomes. And many such endeavors, once discerned, are "swept under the rug" and become among the best kept secrets and are often ultimately dispelled, if not discreetly co-opted. But, the assertion of such endeavors is essential, for precarious is the efficacy of policy for African Americans which is subject to control by Euro-American philosophy and politics. Comprehensive efforts are required to deal with a comprehensive and pervasive phenomenon. Educator Nancy L. Arnez (Howard University) posits that "few, if any, creative solutions" to the "overwhelming problems" of desegregated/integrated education have been wrought, perhaps because 1) the "creative minority"

92

most knowledgeable about the "learning styles, culture and social, educational and psychological needs" of Black youth have been "substantially excluded from the policymaking domain," or 2) "only those Blacks molded into white European thinking patterns have been asked to supply solutions" (1978, 29).

Happily, the changing of thinking patterns founded upon the Euro-American perception of reality or knowledge base has become a major concern among many African American Studies scholars, and their surge of assertion will certainly contribute to effective contemporary and future leadership. A primary example of such concern is that expressed by Russell L. Adams (Howard University). Adams urges that African American/Black Studies scholars give priority to their responsibility of "attempting to change perspectives and habits of thought" (1984, 202), even while continuing the work directed toward correcting "the factual record of the black experience" (204).

Moreover, Adams appropriately notes as premature and fairly futile the traditional focus on the "isms" (e.g., Nationalism, Pan-Africanism, Socialism) of political ideology by a number of African American Studies scholars. Instead, "Black Studies professionals should," Adams submits, "direct their energies and talents toward reshaping the epistemic or perceptual foundations of social thought in America" (202). The fundamental question in this reshaping, Adams posits, is "What is the process through which humans claim to know and how can they verify their claims to knowledge?" In twentieth century terms, Adams points out, this is a basic question of the sociology of knowledge-- of epistemology (204).

Of course, even in traditionally/predominantly Black

93

institutions, Adams notes, the European "epistemic legacy" (207) has prevailed. It is critical that Black America, from a perspective presumably informed by a continuum of information and ideas rooted in a framework which transcends the dominant society's epistemic legacy, intensify its efforts to develop and institutionalize means of deciphering, codifying, and confronting its experience in this society and the experience of the broader African diaspora.

Significant scholarly work has been emerging during the past two decades to fill some philosophical voids about differences in cultural and epistemic underpinnings (e.g., Frye 1975; Karenga 1978; Asante 1980). With regard to William E. Cross' 1991 *Shades of Black, The Chronicle of Higher Education* quotes him as saying that this work is, "as much about the sociology of knowledge as about being Black" (Raymond, A5). Another psychologist, Edwin J. Nichols, has developed a set of delightfully illuminating "philosophical constructs," which he submits account for the behavior and thought processes of three ethnic/racial groupings (1976).

Several examples illustrate Nichols' system. Nichols posits that the traditional European and Euro-American value system, or axiology, places the highest value on "the object or the acquisition of the object," while the traditional African and "Afro-American," Hispanic, and Native American axiology places the highest value on the "interpersonal relationship." An Asian grouping, which also includes Native Americans, places the highest value on the "cohesiveness of the group." Nichols contrasts European-based and African-based logic, describing the first as "dichotomous"--"either/or," and the African-based as "diunital"--couched in the "union of opposites." For Asians, he submits, the philosophical system "Nyaya" defines the essence of logic: "the objective world is conceived independent of thought and mind." Nichols' model--"The Philosophical Aspects of Cultural Difference"--is practicably applicable in many cross-cultural contexts and assists in explaining/understanding the roots of "soul" (African American culture) as well as of other cultural groups. One of the practical applications is his explanation of some of the Black-on-Black violence, which often stems, he posits, from a fractured "relationship" between individuals.

There have been, of course, some perceptive and tenacious avant garde African American educators imbued with a "functional" African American perspective who have committed themselves to tackling "overwhelming problems" of desegregated/integrated education. In *The Besieged School Superintendent* (1987), Arnez has chronicled the efforts of one "creative minority" committed to effecting "a viable educational program" for Black students. The work is a case study of the conflict between Barbara A. Sizemore, the second Black superintendent of the District of Columbia Public School System (1973-75), and the D.C. school board. Sizemore was fired by the school board as the result of her efforts during a short-lived, but tumultuous, tenure in which she sought to decentralize the system and institute a "multilingual, multi-cultural, multi-modal educational plan" (xii) that would provide "educational justice" for all students in the school system in which Blacks were a significant majority (168). Arnez's study is of particular interest to the writer, for it not only chronicles Sizemore's efforts to apply "creative solutions," but also analyzes the "superintendent-school board conflict" within a socio-political context which Arnez describes as not unlike a colonial milieu. Arnez explains:

> In this study, one concern is with the Black elite who have internalized white middle-class values to such an extent that they, too, participate in the subjugation of poor Black people--as illustrated in their support of the status quo (power structure) which denies Blacks their rights and privileges to self-determination (power resources). This elite also sustains and reinforces racial stratification among Black people.

Black leaders in D.C., depending upon white financial support to their campaigns, submitted to what is known in the field of colonial administration as a system of "indirect rule." Some Black leaders have supported, on the whole, the ideas of their white benefactors concerning the educational question. (35) Sizemore has done a study of successful application of viable educational programs for African American children in the Pittsburgh Public School System--success she terms "an abashing anomaly" for the system at large (1988).

Sizemore credits the development of high-achieving Black students in formerly low-achieving schools in significant part to strong African American leadership which was willing to "disagree with superior officers around the choices of routines," as well as materials, "and their implementation" (244-45). One of the "few" earlier (1970) attempts to effect linkage to African American community traditions for African Americans in predominantly White settings of higher education has been described by Atkinson and Hord as espousing a philosophy of "internal separatism/external integration." Application of such a philosophy in schools or colleges is not easy to accomplish or to sustain. Atkinson and Hord purport that this philosophy 1) "embraces Black cultural history/tradition as a framework for strengthening Black racial pride and values and for achieving individual and collective fulfillment while living and learning in White America"; 2) "confronts the American colonial education system's structural realities of elitism, cultural monism, and world Americanization"; and 3) is applicable to informal as well as formal education (1983, 7). The major components of the internal separatism/external integration concept are defined as 1) community--a spirit of Black collectivism, with its corollary of Black unity; 2) cultural pluralism--a state of society in which each race and ethnic group/culture is afforded the continued benefits and development of its original culture while significantly contributing to the larger society and equitably (as needs require) sharing the social benefits and security of that society; 3) internationalism--knowledge of international political realities and a sense of camaraderie of color for the purpose of world humanization. (7)

The aspect of internationalism is cited as imperative; the writers insist that African Americans must not be accomplices in the oppression of other African Americans and other people of color in the world by supporting the exploitative values of American society.

Inherent in the internal separatism/external integration philosophy is the commitment to struggle--to survive, to overcome, to thrive. Black/African American pedagogy must acknowledge struggle as the peren-

97

nial requisite for Black individual and collective fulfillment. A culture of struggle must be assimilated and
perpetuated. Indeed all cultures/peoples must
"struggle," within specific contexts, to survive, to
forge and assert an ethos, to thrive.

The writer is among those who have during the past
decade called for the struggle to continue through
organized African American self-help efforts. At the
1983 national conference of the National Association
for Equal Opportunity in Higher Education (NAFEO),
the writer entreated, during a session presentation as
well as in subsequent communications to NAFEO, and
other groups, including the Congressional Black Caucus:

> Whereas a stable and beneficial system of compre-
> hensive education for the people of the United States
> of America has not yet evolved;
> Whereas the Black people of this country have been
> further victimized by the "victory" of integrated
> education;
> Whereas a liberating system of comprehensive edu-
> cation for the Black people of this country can never
> be a political priority for the ruling class;
> Whereas there can be no self-definition, self-fulfill-
> ment, or even self-preservation for a people without
> self-determination. I propose...that critical Black
> organizations, educators, and spokespersons ally and
> assume forthwith, leadership to formalize the meth-
> odological and directional bases of and the politics
> for implementing a national agenda for the compre-
> hensive education of the Black people of this coun-
> try. (copyright 1984)

During the years succeeding this call for concerted
intervention in the deteriorating condition of African

98

American education, the salience of these enumerated concerns has heightened. Prompted by two consecutive years of calls by attendees at the Congressional Black Caucus (CBC) Legislative Weekend, the 1991 CBC Education Braintrust workshops were devoted to the creation of a National Citizens Commission on African American Education. This action could become a significant effort in the education of African Americans. The 100-member Commission includes "professional educators, teachers, parents, students, civil rights leaders, business persons, and other segments of the African-American community (Owens Announces, 1991)". This national body (although not yet undergirded by Congressional legislation) is to accomplish two basic objectives:

- To provide a critical review of existing national education policy while offering alternative national education policies and strategies for the benefit of African American children.

- To provide national guidance to the African American community for educational policies, strategies, programs and practical activities, to stimulate mobilizations for education in African American communities all over America.

Pointing to the urgent "need for national leadership to confront the conspiracy which is attempting to make African American children invisible," Education Braintrust Chairman Congressman Major Owens (D-NY) indicates that the Commission will focus in particular on what he terms "the 'education emergency' of cuts in the federal budget for education and the impact of proposed national education testing on African American children as recommended'' in the Bush administration's proposed national education initiative (1991) America 2000. Congressman Owens characterizes America 2000 as ''a brightly colored but empty cookie jar where African American children are concerned'' (Owens Announces, 1991).

Indeed, it appears that for African Americans, the problem of ''internal integration'' vs. ''external integration'' will crest by the 21st century (Atkinson and Hord, 20). If African Americans would be free of psychological occupation, educator Paulo Freire's conclusion about the dominated's ''interiorization'' of the ''dominators' cultural models'' might well be heeded:

The dominated can eject the dominators only by getting distance from them and objectifying them. Only then can they recognize them as their antithesis. (1985, 53).

Mitigating the Schoolhouse Effect

The foregoing analysis of the plight of Black America and the call for resolute action would probably evoke a resounding ''Amen!'' from masses of African Americans. But, the need is for the masses of African Americans to move from the Amen Corner to the Action Arena. Vis-a-vis the irony of the schoolhouse effect, resulting from the colonizer's interests/meanings reflected in the language and implementation of *Brown*, which actually facilitated continued psychological occupation of African Americans, African Americans must galvanize around the resolve to decolonize the Black psyche, to arrest further deracination and dehumanization of Black America. All indications are that in many desegregated/integrated settings of education and other institutions of socialization, for African Americans, it is the psyche/soul that suffers most. As

Margaret Walker's poem "For My People" insists, Black America must "take control" of itself (1942, 14). In this spirit, the writer offers the following suggestions, certainly not as "the" answer, but as earnest ponderings about the need for an ongoing struggle by "my people."

- Black America must audaciously forge and institutionalize an effort to promote decolonization of the African American psyche. This effort must not be another Black "nova"--like a star that suddenly becomes a thousand times brighter and then gradually fades, but rather, it must burn eternally intensely. This psychological intervention must have the intensity of the Underground Railroad movement which secretly helped slaves to physical freedom, although it will, of necessity, be more overt.

- This effort must be defined, financed, executed, and sustained by united African Americans who will sound a discreet call to arms and wage an untiring war to empower Black America with the necessary means of self-determination to achieve a people-saving goal.

- This effort must confront those African Americans who either do not comprehend the problem or who choose to arm themselves with a facade of incomprehension for their own selfish gain; it must deal with those African Americans who, drinking from the gourd of the "good life," are relinquishing the sword of assertion at the ballot box as well as in the arena of everyday affairs.

- This effort must be the first phase of a broad, sustained effort and have specific and concrete, measurable, and obtainable objectives--short-

101

range and long-range--which inform and guide its strategies. Those objectives must consist of significant, comprehensive goals transcending all ideologies of Black liberation that are at odds. Those objectives must be intended to free the masses of African Americans from a "domesticating educational practice for one that is liberating" (Freire, 104-105). Those objectives would thus seek to promote among African Americans the realization that buying the rhetoric of individualism and of integration as assimilation is resulting in Blacks being once again "sold down the river," for this rhetoric is articulated by a people who reserve the rights to their racial solidarity and cultural continuity as necessary tools to sustain the colonized condition of African Americans.

- This effort must seek to arrest what Carter G. Woodson in 1933 termed the "miseducation" of a people who thus "unconsciously contribute to their own undoing by perpetuating the regime of the oppressor" (xxxi).

- This effort must undergird the African American's quest to dissolve what DuBois termed "double-consciousness, this sense of always looking at one's self through the eyes of others, of measuring one's soul by the tape of a world that looks on in amused contempt and pity" (1961, 16-17). There must be forged a "new," collective double-consciousness, similar to that of the philosophy of internal separatism/external integration described above, which resists the employment of Black minds against Black people (Atkinson and Hord, 2).

- This effort must strive to increase the presence

of "functional" African American educators in all levels of schooling, including educators in key decision-making positions. These educators must be sensitive to and willing to implement measures that promote the welfare of all racial and ethnic groups as well as persons of different sexes. The decline in the presence of Black males--who would have critical knowledge of the psychological and cultural needs of young Black males--in both elementary and secondary schools is a significant factor in serious problems of failure, pushout and dropout rates for African American males. The Office of Minority concerns of the American Council on Education reported in 1988 that only 1.2 percent of elementary and 3.2 percent of secondary school teachers were Black men (12). But whatever the race or sex of educators in our schools, they must have the capacity for bonding with whatever the race or sex of their students, in a healthy, supportive manner that fosters students' desire to successfully sustain their education. Too many students experience rejection and alienation.

• African American educators must comprehend and defend the necessity for racial and ethnic groups in this pluralistic society to exercise essential control of the "significant environment and psychological factors impinging" upon them (Appleton 1983, 10), for cultural well-being and preservation. Such control in the schoolhouse is of unequivocal importance in the promotion of cultural well-being. And it is in the schoolhouse that African American educators, students and their parents receive often overwhelming resis-

103

tance to their assertion of cultural philosophy--
of their world view--which is the foundation of
sustenance, motivation, and developmental security for Black youth.

- This effort must bridge the ''wide gulf between
academia and the avenue'' (Burns, in LoLordo
1984, G3) and reach out to the so-called African
American ''underclass'' on the streets--those
most threatened by genocide--as well as to African American children and adults in schools,
colleges and churches. A now dispersed and
insidiously class-conscious Black America must
strive to recapture those strengths and advantages of the Black neighborhoods where Black
families--of all social strata--and other Black
institutions comprised a committed, nurturing
network. There must be waged a comprehensive
propaganda campaign, which uses media and
tactics appropriate for the times and for the task
at hand, intended to rejuvenate the potential for
systematic, concerted social and political action
and clout among all ''strata'' of African Americans. Indeed, institutionalization of an African
American creed, or litany, that instructed the
young and served as a stabilizing and motivating
force for all African Americans would not be out
of order in the struggle to reverse the accelerated
deterioration of a people's striving together,
''with one mind,'' in the face of contemporary,
more sophisticated forms of oppression.

- This effort must pull out all stops to provide
preventive and corrective instruction for African
American youth--individual and collective survival savvy as well as academic skills, in the

international as well as the national context--
from the schoolroom to the board room. Prominent African American performers and other
artists, business persons, writers, publishers and
other media personalities, must assume more
responsible roles in this effort. Also, African
American "great books" (Hilliard, 1970-1986),
rather than being hidden treasures, must be lo-
cated and circulated not only from school and
college and public libraries but from church,
"lodge," and poolroom libraries. All of these
sources must support literary discussion groups
to stimulate interest and expedite understanding
in this long neglected and often demeaned area
of instruction.

- This effort must restore the tradition of the arts
as a central force in the development/nurturance
of the African American psyche/soul. These arts
are the embodiment of the collective history/
experience and ethos of the African American
people and they therefore promote collective
consciousness and cultural memory and purpose, as well as aesthetic definition and fulfillment. An example is the African American (Negro) spiritual, a genre of music all but unknown
to contemporary youth, that was for almost two
centuries a source of subliminal instruction about
the significance of struggle and tenacity, of morality, of overcoming oppression, of family and
community, as well as a concrete source of consola-
tion and emotional release and reinforcement
(Lovell 1972, 274). And with each new stage of
the ambivalent African sojourn in America, new
sacred and secular artistic forms emerged, par-

105

ticularly oral/aural forms, "soulful" vehicles for coping with an oppressed status. Poet and novelist Al Young has been quoted as stating: "And for everything they took away, we came up with something new....We sang some new songs, and danced us some new dances....See, you can put a hurting on the body, but you can't touch the soul" (cited in Pasteur and Toldson 1982, 3). But, has the current forfeiting of identity, community and cultural continuity effected a critical void in the heretofore creative and expressive coping capacity of African Americans? Or are the messages of the emerging musical form of "rap" to be the critical stimulant for coping with and, perhaps, overcoming contemporary oppression?

- African American youth must be afforded structured "survival" instruction by insightful, unintimidated African Americans. This would include instruction in the chronology of the African diaspora, and such concepts as Nichols' "Philosophical Aspects of Cultural Difference" (1976), particularly the significant difference in European and Euro-American value systems and the African and African American value systems. Such insight is critical for survival in the workplace as well as in social settings to assist in the need for delicate balancing of the Eurocentric world view and the Africentric world view, a balancing so critical to the individual as well as collective well-being of African Americans. Some Euro-American values, after all, seem undergirding factors in racism and other forms of conquest and subjugation. Individualism and competitiveness appear to be behaviors which

106

facilitate the quest for the "object."

- This instruction would also communicate knowledge about the historically thematic and repetitive nature of White domination/manipulation of Black thought and action, with particular attention to an analysis of oppression in the desegregated/integrated 1970s and 1980s as compared to prior eras. It would examine the import of intra-group as well as inter-group relationships. Microcosms of the larger society, desegregated/integrated higher education settings are pregnant with situations to be cited, analyzed, and confronted.

- African American educators who are willing to join the forces, but are not themselves adequately informed, must gear up in the interest of their constituents and the cause. Millions of Black students silently weep vis-`a-vis the lack of understanding and assistance from those who should be their cultural mentors. White students generally do not appear to be lacking development of understanding of the basic tenets of the status, purpose, and direction of their cohesive group.

- African Americans must become better informed about the many guises of "contemporary racism" (Kinloch 1985, 42). Under whatever cloaks it lurks, the effect of repression and/or oppression--usually based on race--is the same, and often more pernicious. African Americans--and all Americans--must become familiar with studies of the psychological factors involved in racist behavior such as Hilliard between 1970-1986: noted "denial of reality"; "perceptual distortions"; "delusions of grandeur" (superiority);

"phobias in the face of differences"; "project-
ing blame" (blaming the victim). Hilliard also
describes the various means by which the subjugation of a people or social group can be effected:
erasing cultural memory; teaching the supremacy
of the controlling group; controlling institutions
of socialization, thereby preventing the suppressed group from educating themselves realis-
tically and sending "messages" among themselves; controlling resources and wealth; physi-
cally segregating the suppressed group. Black
youth are alarmingly oblivious to the operation
of seemingly benign or ostensibly "all-Ameri-
can" principles, which may be actually harmful
to collective welfare, e.g., "equal opportunity"
measures (Kinloch, 43) which are often intended
to counteract Affirmative Action and to impact
negatively on Black individual and collective
self-help, self-determination, and opportunity
for meaningful advancement.

- African Americans must, when individual and
collective well-being are clearly threatened, reject participation in schools and colleges/univer-
sities and any organizations that are unwilling to
or inadequately prepared to project genuine
multicultural perspectives. African Americans
must not be rendered unable to go home again.
- Black America must accelerate the rate at which
it is becoming disillusioned with the Constitution of the United States of America as an instrument to guarantee equality and, indeed, with the
tacit "checks and balances" in the total gover-
nance system which wield the Constitution as a
double-edged sword of disguised economic,

political, social, and cultural oppression of African Americans. This same Constitution has been used by states even in early African American history to rule group social and economic "self-help" endeavors by its Black citizenry (Carson 1987,4).

- Black America must galvanize its forces to push for unconditional Congressional legislation which will make unconstitutional any discrimination against the culture of a minority group, based on race, as well as economic and political discrimination, as social historian Harold Cruse has suggested (1987, 381). Cruse recommends that this legislation would be warranted if the Equal Rights Amendment (ERA) is ratified, which proposes that discrimination against women, as a class, be illegal. However, the writer suggests that this action is in order whether or not the ERA is ratified (recommendation submitted at the Congressional Black Caucus Educational Braintrust/Legislative Weekend, 1988).

- All else failing, this effort might approach the United Nations Assembly to plead its cause and request an investigation of the United States of America in its treatment of racial minorities (also submitted to the CBC, 1988). Black America must raise the question of the failure of the U.S. Senate to ratify the UN's Covenants on Economic and Social Rights, even though President Carter signed the Covenants in 1977 (Raskin 1986, 198). Political Scientist Y.N. Kly has noted in his enlightening work *International Law and the Black Minority in the U.S.* that not as of his writing had the Congress ratified even the UN Genocide treaty (1985, 36), the Convention on the Prevention and Punishment of the Crime of Genocide having been adopted by the UN in 1948 (33). That treaty was finally ratified in the last session of Congress in 1988 (Knutson 1988, A11), but with a disclaimer: the U.S. will not recognize the International Court of Justice. Not surprisingly, little media coverage has accompanied the long-overdue action. By UN definition, genocide has many faces (Kly, 33). The momentum of the devastating phenomena perpetrated against African Americans in this society, skillfully adapted and reinforced during the past several decades, has ensured the psychological domination and/or physical demise of millions of this racial group, has ensured a significant decline of African Americans as a cultural, political, economic, social, and even physical entity: unemployment; poverty; disease; military exploitation; miseducation; mal-education; criminal orientation; incarceration; chemical addiction--dehumanization.

As in prior eras of African American oppression, the male remains the primary victim of this physical, psychological, and economic assault by the dominant society. Educator-lecturer Jawanza Kunjufu is one who advances the theory that the worsening plight of school-age African American males is the result of a conspiratorial effort to "destroy Black boys." For many African Americans, the overall plight of the African American male lends credibility to such a theory. Whatever the scenario, the *Brown* fallout has affected conditions of African American education and of other dominant institutions of socialization which facilitate the cycle of assault and the consequent decline of the number of capable African American men for positions of leadership in the home, in schools and colleges, and in society at large. Grave consequences of destructive forces are manifest in such statistics as presented in 1990 by The Sentencing Project (Marc Mauer) which indicate that almost one of every four African American males between 20 and 29 years of age is either imprisoned or under some form of criminal justice jurisdiction.

Some may ask how likely it is that Black America will effect a plan that will foster significant self-determination within the American system of desegregation/integration of public education. Spurred by the experience of increasingly devastating circumstances and overt as well as covert discriminatory acts in the decade of the 80s, more critical thinking and action have already begun to emerge from the African American community. But, the question is not how likely it is that a viable plan will be effected; African Americans must be concerned about what will occur if such a plan is not put into place: the material and spiritual demise of African Americans. The fruition of such a plan would be neither instant nor panacean, but the struggle for its realization should at least serve to galvanize the thinking of African Americans about the realities of defining (beyond physical characteristics) and sustaining peoplehood--or about the consequences of consciously or unconsciously relinquishing peoplehood. And without the realization of such a plan, the cycle of assault on the African American psyche/soul is unlikely to be broken.

EPILOGUE

As external cold war forces increasingly pushed this country in the fifties and sixties to finally live its creed of democracy, and the internal forces of African Americans increasingly pushed to make their world safe from previous practice of democracy, American institutions shifted their form of Black containment from segregated neocolonialism to integrated neocolonialism. Almost a century of the segregated form had firmly established the prudence of training and employing the colonized elite to further secure the material inequities of economic, political, and social oppression and to perpetrate the racist dominant meanings of the colonizer. However, for almost two generations now, we have witnessed the even larger devastations of African Americans, as so many of our elite reflect the ascendant cultural hierarchies in this era of integrated neocolonialism. Although historical events are finally only markers we use to identify movements rather than being determinative, the *Brown vs. Board of Education* Supreme Court decision of 1954 increased Black contact with White institutions and access to their mainstreams, and contributed to a further shifting in our cultural repression toward an American identity and ethos.

The author of this groundbreaking work, Pansye S.

Atkinson, showed us clearly that institutional arrangements and meanings of the dominant elite can be let out enough to project openendedness, while further ensconcing power. Perhaps the most persuasive subtlety of the ''progressive'' civil rights arrangements was/is its management of African Americans.

The reader discovered a number of useful insights in this analysis which provide imperatives for changing Black individual and collective behavior. First, there are heuristic advantages in the internal colonialism model, which Atkinson chooses to demystify, the institutional nature of our historical and contemporary oppression. Focusing on education, she demonstrated that the nature and extent of cultural capital available to Blacks reinforce cultural repression and economic exploitation, which contribute to vulnerability to political control and physical repression. Such institutional subjugations become clear dimensions of confusion about identity and values systems, growing class cleavages, and additional permanent impoverishment.

The author admitted that African Americans were assaulted by institutional arrangements before *Brown,* but convincingly asserts that many current Black dislocations and ravages can be best understood by the ''legacies of *Brown*''. We are more American than we have ever been; we have abysmal poverty than ever before.

But although Atkinson insisted that African Americans recognize that our present plight is not essentially one of personal prejudices, nor our unprecedented middle-class ''successes'' ones of unmitigated personal triumphs, she did not leave us languishing in despair. Rather, the author proposed that we contend with the new configuration of our oppression with

113

institutional strategies. We are no strangers to our own institutions; even as recently as the sixties and early seventies, we attempted to modify and strengthen old institutions, and to build new ones. But one legacy of *Brown* has been the de-emphasis on Black institutions; too many of us were sure that they were no longer needed, and/or were in fact, anachronisms. We were dangerously wrong, and warnings of greater disasters seem to be everywhere. This last lesson of blind optimism and misdirected faith has been the most difficult one, because the ranks of leaderships have more color than ever before.

The author would conclude that our pain at their disaffection must be matched by the determination to reconfigure our own leadership. The logic of integrated neocolonialism is unfeeling. Not only do individual ''success'' stories no longer count unless they collapse into our collective progress, but they murderously tally for the colonizer.

This book arrives at a moment when some African Americans are becoming believers again. Caught up in the trailing euphoric dark mist of government appointments as well as in the burgeoning numbers of Black managers on Capitol Hill, they talk once more of new days acomin'. This reminds us all of the immense costs of such lightness before. This is no time for false self-congratulations; there is time only for developing Black institutions to contend with the deepening assaults described here, and thus to resist our own mystification and dehumanization. As the only African American author of a full-length work--*Reconstructing Memory*--which employs an internal colonialism model to use Black literature to make a cultural critique for the

114

reordering of Black political objectives, I welcome this kindred analysis of our objective condition as yet a nation within a nation.

Fred Lee Hord, Ph.D.
Founder/President
National Association for Black Culture Centers

REFERENCES

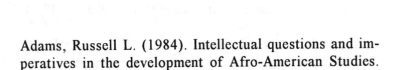

Adams, Russell L. (1984). Intellectual questions and imperatives in the development of Afro-American Studies. The Journal of Negro Education, 53 201-225.

Adams v. Richardson, 480 F. 2nd 1159 (D.C. Cir. 1973).

Akbar, Na'im. (1984). Chains and images of psychological slavery. Jersey City, N.J.: New Mind Productions.

Allen, Robert L. (1970). Black awakening in capitalist America: an analytic history. Garden City, N.Y.: Anchor Books/Doubleday.

Alkalimat, Abdul and Associates. (1986). Introduction to Afro-American studies: A people's college primer. Chicago: Twenty-first Century Books and Publications. Originally published 1973.

Appleton, Nicholas. (1983). Cultural pluralism in education: Theoretical foundations. New York & London: Longman.

Arnez, Nancy L. (1978). Implementation of desegregation as a discriminatory process. The Journal of Negro Education, 48, 28-57.

Arnez, Nancy L. (1981). The besieged school superintendent. Washington: University Press of America.

Asante, Molefi Kete. (1980). Afrocentricity--The theory of social change. Buffalo: Amulefi Publishing Co.

Atkinson, Pansye S. (1983). Proposal regarding the education of Black youth in the United States of America. Copyright 1984. Included in Atkinson and Hord, 1983, pp. 19-20.

Atkinson, Pansye S. & Hord, Fred L. (1986). The BEST System: Black academic and cultural retention: (Save the children). ERIC Document Reproduction Service. No. ED 261 563. Also available from PANFRE Productions, P.O. Box 77, Frostburg, MD 21532 (1983, revised 1988).

Ayers v. Mabus, United States Law Week 6588 (1992).

Baldwin, Joseph A. (1985). Psychological aspects of European cosmology in American society. The Western Journal of Black Studies, 9, 216-223.

Bell, Derrick. (1979). Learning from the Brown experience. The Black Scholar, 11 (1), 9-16.

Bell, Derrick (1980). Brown and the interest-convergence dilemma. In Derrick Bell (Ed.), Shades of Brown (pp. 91-106). New York & London: Teachers College Press.

Bell, Derrick. The hidden danger in the Clarence Thomas appointment. Newsday. Excerpt from article published. Actual quote deleted.

Bennett, Lerone Jr. (1975). The shaping of Black America. Chicago: Johnson Publishing Company. The essays in this book appeared in Ebony magazine between 1972 and 1975.

117

Billingsley, Andrew (1971). Foreword. In Robert B. Hill The strengths of black families. New York: Emerson Hall Publishers.

Black Olivet students leave school over racial incidents. (1992, April 23). Black Issues in Higher Education, p. 3.

Bolling v. Sharpe, 347 U.S. 497 (1954).

Bonacich, Edna. (1988). Race and class in the inner city {Review of the truly disadvantaged: the inner city, the underclass, and public policy} Without prejudice, 2 (1), 82-89.

Borger, Gloria. (1992, November 16). The storming of Capitol Hill. Newsweek, pp. 64-66.

Boxhill, Bernard R. (1983). Self-respect and protest. In Leonard Harris (Ed.), Philosophy born of struggle (pp. 190-198). Dubuque: Kendall/Hunt.

Briggs v. Elliott, 98 F. Supp. 529 (1951).

Brown v. Board of Education of Topeka, 98 F. Supp. 797 (1951).

Brown v. Board of Education of Topeka, 347 U.S. 483 (1954) (Brown I).

Brown v. Board of Education of Topeka, 349 U.S. 294 (1955) (Brown II).

Bureau of the Census. (1991, August). Poverty in the United States: 1990, Current population reports: consumer income, (Series P-60, No. 175) Washington D.C.: U.S. Department of Commerce, Economics and Statistics administration.

Carson, Emmett D. (1987). Despite long history, black philanthropy gets little credit as "self-help" tool. <u>Focus.</u> The Joint Center for Political Studies, 15 (6), 3-7 passim.

Carter, Deborah J. & Wilson, Reginald (1992, January). <u>Minorities in higher education</u>, 1991, Tenth annual status report. Washington D.C.: American Council on Education.

Carter, Robert L. (1980). A reassessment of Brown v. Board. In Derrick Bell (Ed.), <u>Shades of Brown</u> (pp. 21-28). New York and London: Teachers College Press.

Clark, Kenneth. (1965). <u>Dark ghetto: Dilemmas of social power.</u> New York: Harper & Row.

Clark, Kenneth B. (1955). <u>Prejudice and your child.</u> Boston: Beacon Press.

Congressional Black Caucus Foundation 20th Annual Legislative Weekend. (1990, September). <u>Endangered African American males, Part II: Higher education road blocks and obstacles on the way up.</u> Fact sheet for session convened by Congressman Major Owens.

Cross, William E. (1991). <u>Shades of black: Diversity in African American identity.</u> Philadelphia: Temple University press.

Cruse, Harold. (1968). <u>Rebellion or revolution?</u> New York: William Morrow. The essay related to colonialism cited in this book originated in 1962.

Cruse, Harold. (1987). <u>Plural but equal.</u> New York: William Morrow.

Davis v. County School Board of Prince Edward County. 103 F. Supp. 337 (1952).

Domhoff, G. William. (1967). Who rules America? Englewood Cliffs, N.J.: Prentice-Hall.

Douglass, Frederick. (1973). Narrative of the life of Frederick Douglass--An American slave. Garden City: Doubleday. Original publisher: Anti-slavery Office, Boston, 1845.

Dred Scott v. Sanford, 19 Howard 393 (1857).

DuBois, W.E. Burghardt. (1961). The souls of black folk. Greenwich, CT: Fawcett Publications. Original publisher: A.C. McClurg & Co., Chicago, 1903.

Duke, Lynne. (1992, September 27). Two-earner black families record income gains. The Washington Post, p. A13.

Fanon, Frantz. (1963). The wretched of the earth. New York: Grove Press.

Fanon, Frantz. (1967). Black skin, white masks. New York: Grove Press. Originally published in 1952.

Fanon, Frantz. (1969). Toward the African revolution. New York: Grove Press.

Fleming, Jacqueline. (1984). Blacks in college. San Francisco, Washington, & London: Jossey-Bass.

Frazier, E. Franklin. (1939). The Negro family in the United States. Chicago: University of Chicago Press.

Freire, Paulo. (1985). The politics of education: culture, power and liberation. Translated by Henry A. Giroux. Granby, Mass: Bergin & Garvey Publishers, Inc.

Frye, Charles. (1975). Towards a philosophy of Black studies. San Francisco: R&E Associates.

Gould, Steven Jay. (1979, December). "The father of Jensenism." [Review of Cyril Burt, psychologist]. Psychology Today, 104-106.

Griggs v. Duke Power, 401 U.S. 424 (1971).

Guthrie, Robert V. (1980). "The psychology of Black Americans: A historical perspective." In Reginald L. Jones (Ed.), Black Psychology (pp. 13-22). New York: Harper & Row.

Haney, James E. (1978). "The effects of the Brown decision on Black educators." The Journal of Negro Education, 47, 88-95.

Hart, Phillip S. (1984). Institutional effectiveness in the production of Black baccalaureates. Atlanta: Southern Education Foundation.

Hayes, Floyd W. III. (1981). Structures of dominance and the political economy of Black higher education in a technocratic era: A theoretical framework. (Occasional Paper No. 3). Washington, D.C.: Howard University, Institute for the Study of Educational Policy.

Hentoff, Nat (1982, August 23). The Integrationist. The New Yorker, pp. 37-73 passim.

Hill, Robert B., (1991). The strengths of black families. New York: Emerson Hall.

Hilliard, Asa Grant III. (1970-1986). Free your mind: Return to the source, African origins {Video tape}. West Productions, P.O. Bos 911253, East Point, GA 330364

Hord, Fred. (1974). Black one is many? In Fred Hord, After (h)ours (pp. 15-16). Chicago: Third World Press.

121

Hord, Fred Lee (1988). Metaphorical and metamorphical Black literary criticism: A pedagogical model (Doctoral dissertation, The Union for Experimenting Colleges and Universities, 1987). University Microfilms International Dissertation Information Service, 48, 2337A.

Howie, Donald L. W. (1973). The image of Black people in Brown v. Board of Education. The Journal of Black Studies, 3, 371-384.

Jaschik, Scott. (1990, July 5). Appeals court dismisses landmark lawsuit on college desegregation. The Chronicle of Higher Education, 1A, 22A.

Jaynes, Gerald & Williams, Robin M., Jr. (Eds.). (1989) A common destiny. Washington D.C.: National Academy Press.

Jensen, Arthur R. (1969). How can we boost IQ and scholastic achievement? Harvard Educational Review, 29, 1-123.

Jordan, Vernon. (1971). Preface. In Robert B. Hill The strengths of black families. New York: Emerson Hall Publishers.

Kardiner, Abram & Ovesey, Lionel. (1951). The mark of oppression. New York: Norton.

Karenga, Maulana. (1978). Essays on struggle: position and analysis. San Diego: Kawaida Publications.

Karenga, Maulana. (1982). Introduction to Black studies. Los Angeles: Kawaida Publications.

Kennedy, Paul. (1989). The rise and fall of great powers. New York: Vintage Books.

122

Kinloch, Graham C. (1985). "Contemporary forms of racism." The Western Journal of Black Studies, 9, 40-45.

Kluger, Richard. (1977). Simple justice. New York: Vintage Books. Original publisher, Alfred A. Knopf, Inc., 1976.

Kly, Y.N. (1985). International law and the black minority in the U.S. Atlanta: Clarity/Commoners'.

Knutson, Lawrence. (1988, October 15). Senate finishes action on outlawing genocide. The Washington Post, 11A.

Kunjufu, Jawanza. (1983). Countering the conspiracy to destroy black boys, Vol. I. Chicago: African American Images.

Kunjufu, Jawanza. (1986). Countering the conspiracy to destroy black boys, Vol. II. Chicago: African American Images.

LoLordo, Ann. (1984, May 13). Black middle class faces problems of Black family. The Sun, p. 3G.

Lovell, John Jr. (1972). Black Song: The forge and the flame. New York: Paragon House.

Malcolm X. (1965). The autobiography of Malcolm X. New York: Grove Press.

Manner, Joshua, Foote, Donna, & Manly, Howard. (1992, May).L.A.--what's next: Black on the block. Newsweek, pp. 40-41, 44.

Marable, Manning. (1985, February). "In search of the "new" Booker T. Editorial Commentary: On the QT." The National Leader, 3 (7) p. 26.

McLaurin v. Oklahoma, State Regents 339 U.S. 637 (1950).

Miller, LeMar P. (1980). Testing Black students: Implications for assessing inner-city schools. In Reginald L. Jones (Ed.), Black psychology, (pp. 165-176). New York: Harper & Row. Originally published in 1975 in The Journal of Negro Education, 44.

Milloy, Courtland. (1991, July 14). Conflicting images of Clarence Thomas. The Washington Post, p. d3.

National Commission on Excellence in Education.(1983, April). A nation at risk: The imperative for educational reform. A report to the nation and the Secretary of Education. Washington, D.C.: U.S. Dept. of Education.

Mohr, Paul B. (1977). The Adams Case Dateline: 1977. Washington, D.C.: National Association for Equal Opportunity (NAFEO).

NAACP, Washington Bureau. (1991, August 13). Talking points on the Nomination of Judge Clarence Thomas for the United States Supreme Court. Washington D.C.

National Commission on Exellence in Education. (1983, April). A nation at risk: The imperative for educational reform. A. D.C.: U.S. Dept. of Education.

Newby, Robert G. (1979). "Desegregation--Its inequities and paradoxes." The Black Scholar, 11 (1), 17-68 passim.

Nichols, Edwin J. (1976). Nichols' model: The philosophical aspects of cultural difference. Available from Edwin J. Nichols,1523 Underwood Street, N.W., Washington, D.C. 20012.

Nieman, Donald G. (1991). Promises to keep: African Americans and the constitutional order, 1776 to the present. New York: Oxford University Press.

Olivet president says he will resign. (1992, May 13). The Chronicle of Higher Education, p. A4.

Owens announces formation of National Citizens Commission on African-American Education. (1991, September). Congressman Major Owens, News Release.

Panati, Charles with MacPherson, Malcolm. (1976, December 20). An epitaph for Sir Cyril? Newsweek, p. 76.

Pasteur, Alfred B. & Toldson, Ivory L. (1982). Roots of soul. Garden City, N.Y.: Anchor Press/Doubleday.

Plessy v. Ferguson, 163 U.S. 537 (1896).

Raskin, Marcus G. (1986). The common good--its politics, policies, and philosophy. New York & London: Routledge & Kegan Paul.

Ravitch, Diane. (1980). Desegregation--varieties of meaning. In Derrick Bell (Ed.), Shades of Brown (pp. 31-47). New York & London: Teachers College Press.

Raymond, Chris. (1991. May 8). Cornell scholar attacks key psychological studies thought to demonstrate blacks self-hatred. The Chronicle of Higher Education, A5, A10-11.

Reynolds, Barbara. (1985, March 6). "Inquiry: Discrimination [Interview with Clarence M. Pendleton]. "U.S. Today, 11A.

Saving the African American child. (1984, November). A Report of the Task Force on Black Academic and Cultural Retention. Washington, D.C.: National Alliance of Black School Educators, Inc. Research team headed by Asa G. Hilliard, III and Barbara A. Sizemore.

Sipuel v. University of Oklahoma Law School, 332 U.S. 631 (1948).

Sizemore, Barbara A. (1986). "The madison elementary school: A turnaround case." The Journal of Negro Education. 57, 243-266.

Staples, Robert. (June, 1976). "Race and colonialism." The Black Scholar, 7 (9), 37-49.

Stephan, Walter. (1978, March). School desegregation: An evaluation of predictions made in Brown v. Board of Education. In Psychology Bulletin. 85, 217-238.

St. John, Nancy. (1975). School desegregation: Outcomes for children. New York: John Wiley & Sons.

Sweatt v. Painter, 339 U.S. 629 (1950).

Tabb, William K. (1970). The political economy of the black ghetto. New York: W.W. Norton & Co., Inc.

Tillman, James A. Jr., & Tillman, Mary Norman. (1972). Black intellectuals, White liberals and race relations: An Analytic Overview. Phylon, 33, 54-66.

Turner, James. (1977 March/April). Black America: Colonial economy under siege. First World, 1 (2), 7-9.

Walker, Margaret. (1942). For my people. In Margaret Walker, For my people (pp. 13-14). New Haven: Yale University Press.

Weinberg, Meyer. (1983). The search for quality integrated Education. Westport, CT & London: Greenwood Press.

White, Joseph L. (1980). Toward a Black psychology. In Reginald L. Jones (Ed.), <u>Black psychology</u> (pp. 5-12). New York: Harper & Row. Originally published in <u>Ebony</u> magazine, 1970 September.

White, Joseph L., Parham, William D., & Parham, Thomas A. (1980). Black psychology: The Afro-American tradition as a unifying force for traditional psychology. In Reginald L. Jones (Ed.), <u>Black Psychology</u> (pp. 56-66). New York: Harper & Row.

Wilson, Reginald and Carter, Deborah J. (1988) <u>Minorities in higher education.</u> Seventh annual status report. (1988). Washington, D.C.: American Council on Education.

Wilson, William Julius. (1978). <u>The declining significance of race: Blacks and changing American institutions.</u> Chicago: University of Chicago Press.

Woodson, Carter G. (1933). <u>Miseducation of the Negro.</u> Washington, D.C.: Associated Publishers.

Wright, Sarah E. (1992). The anti-black agenda. In the <u>Black Scholar</u> (Ed.). Court of Appeal (pp. 225-228). New York: Ballantine Books.

127